MICHAEL JACKSON

LEGEND

1958–2009

Also by Chas Newkey-Burden

Simon Cowell: The Unauthorized Biography
Amy Winehouse: The Biography
Alexandra Burke: A Star Is Born
Heston Blumenthal: The Biography of the World's Most
Brilliant Master Chef
Paris Hilton: Life on the Edge
Not In My Name: A Compendium of Modern Hypocrisy
(with Julie Burchill)

MICHAEL JACKSON

LEGEND

1958–2009

Chas Newkey-Burden

MICHAEL O'MARA BOOKS LIMITED

First published in Great Britain in 2009 by
Michael O'Mara Books Ltd
9 Lion Yard, Tremadoc Road
London SW4 7NQ

A CIP catalogue record for this book is available from the British Library.

Hardback ISBN: 978-1-84317-440-0
Trade paperback ISBN: 978-1-84317-441-7

1 3 5 7 9 10 8 6 4 2

www.mombooks.com

Designed and typeset by e-type

Plates section designed by www.envy.co.uk

Printed and bound in Great Britain by Clays Ltd, St Ives plc

CONTENTS

ACKNOWLEDGEMENTS

As befits a man of his enormous stature and legacy, to research a book about the life of Michael Jackson is a mammoth, overwhelming task. Thank you so much to the usual suspects for their support and encouragement, particularly Chris Morris and Lindsay Davies. Thanks, too, to Ilona Jasiewicz for her meticulous editing.

Numerous books have already been published about the life of Michael Jackson, each with their own appeal and strengths. J. Randy Taraborrelli's *Michael Jackson: The Magic and the Madness* brilliantly reflects the long-term access Taraborrelli enjoyed with the Jackson family and others associated with the story. It is a fine work and proved a particularly helpful source in my research, along with the other books listed in the bibliography.

PICTURE CREDITS

Even before its stirring conclusion, the public memorial for Michael Jackson had been an extraordinary affair, befitting the man in whose memory it was being held. Just three days earlier, America had observed Independence Day, a celebration that brings the people of the nation together. An entirely different kind of event, the public memorial of Michael Jackson would unite people across the entire globe for a few hours. It was one of the most-discussed events of the decade. Over a billion people around the world tuned in to watch the emotional send-off on television, and millions more followed the proceedings online. Whether they were mourning his death, celebrating his life or were simply curious to see how this consummate showman's final performance would proceed, people felt compelled to view.

They watched as, in front of Michael's gold-plated coffin, there were moving orations from family, friends and colleagues, and songs from performers including Stevie Wonder, Mariah Carey and Jennifer Hudson. Michael had himself once predicted, in a typically quirky moment, that his funeral would be the 'greatest show on earth'. Many of his fans would disagree with their hero in a sense because, emotionally charged though the event undoubtedly was, it lacked the one performer who could have instantly guaranteed it 'greatest' status – Michael Jackson, the man who in his life put on more great shows around the world than perhaps any human being in living memory.

But then, just when it seemed that the event was about to end quietly, someone whose voice the world had never heard decided to add her own thoughts to proceedings. The microphone stand was lowered so she could reach it and then she paused, wondering how to find the words that would express how she felt. 'I just wanted to say that ever since I was born, Daddy has been the best father I could imagine,' said Michael's daughter Paris, gripping the microphone with her right hand, and struggling to hold back the tears. 'I just want to say I love him so much,' added the eleven-year-old before breaking down and seeking comfort in the welcoming arms of her aunt Janet.

It was an unexpected but appropriate ending to the memorial ceremony. Suddenly, the memory was not of the 'King of Pop', who sold 750 million albums and wooed audiences worldwide. Nor was it of 'Wacko Jacko', the oddball obsession of the global media who turned from a beautiful black boy into a strange-looking, pale-faced, androgynous adult, the subject of unpleasant suspicions. For a few precious moments, the bitter memories of all the controversies were dissolved by his daughter's tears, and even the legacy of his magnificent music was drowned out by her sobs. Instead, for just a few moments, it was time to reflect upon Michael Jackson the man, about whom so much has been said but so little understood.

Here is the full story of his remarkable life...

CHAPTER ONE

One of Michael Jackson's earliest memories was of lying in the arms of his mother Katherine, listening to her soulful, soprano rendition of the song 'You Are My Sunshine'. In later life he became one of the planet's most discussed celebrities and some of that discussion was very uncomplimentary towards him. But back then, lying as a youngster in his mother's embrace, he heard only the sweetest lyrics, as she sang that he would never know how much she loved him. The song concluded with a heartfelt plea that her 'sunshine' never be taken away from her. Little could mother or son know at the time that her sunshine would be taken away from her, or that an extraordinary life was ahead of him.

* * *

Michael Joseph Jackson was born on the evening of 29 August 1958 in Gary, Indiana. The summer of 1958 was rich in births of future American pop idols. Prince was born in Minnesota in June, and Madonna in Michigan in August, just thirteen days prior to Michael. Three decades later, this trio would rival each other in pop charts across the globe. Michael was the seventh of nine children born to Joseph Walter Jackson and his wife Katherine. Joseph was born in 1929 in Arkansas, the oldest of five children. His own father, Samuel – a strict and stern man – divorced Joseph's mother when Joseph was in his teens. Katherine's parents, too, had divorced during her childhood. Born in 1930 in Alabama, she had one younger sister. By the time the couple met in the 1940s, Joseph had already married and divorced. Soon after he and Katherine met they were engaged and they tied the knot within six months of their engagement. The humble ceremony was held on 5 November 1949 in Crown Point, Indiana.

The newlyweds moved to Gary. With a population of just under 200,000 at the time, and situated some twenty-five miles outside the city of Chicago, Gary was founded in 1906. The employment opportunities there were dominated by the US steel industry. However, the trade was on the brink of a downturn when the Jacksons moved there, and the city was to be hit hard by the declining fortunes of its chief source of commerce. All the same, the Jacksons quickly felt at home in Gary. There was a healthy proportion of African-Americans in the city, which became one of the first in the United States to elect an African-American mayor, Richard G. Hatcher.

The couple's first child, Maureen, also known as Rebbie, was born in 1950. The following year they had their second child, Jackie. Then followed Tariano (to be known as Tito) in 1953, Jermaine LaJuane (1954), LaToya Yvonne (1956) and Marlon David in 1957. After Michael's birth came Steven Randall in 1961 and Janet in 1966. The family was complete, but one of their offspring quickly stood out from the pack. 'Ever since Michael was very young, he seemed different to me from the rest of the children,' remembered his mother Katherine. There were signs of his future career direction when he was as young as eighteen months. Michael, holding a bottle in his hands as if it were a microphone, would joyfully dance round the kitchen. By the time he turned three, he was already singing in front of his grandmother, who recalled his 'beautiful' voice as a 'joy to listen to'. His father was later to say that Michael had wanted to be an entertainer since the age of four. Michael would say in later life, 'I really believe that each person has a destiny from the day he's born and certain people have a thing that they're meant to do.'

* * *

The Jackson family lived in a small clapboard house on a road that has since been renamed Jackson Street in honour of the city's most famous residents. The living arrangements were modest. 'You could take five steps from the front door and you'd be out the back,' said Michael of the property. 'It was really no bigger than a garage.' As such, living conditions were naturally very cramped for such a big family. There were only two bedrooms, and Joseph and Katherine shared one of them. The other was occupied by the five brothers, who slept in a bunk bed with three tiers. Michael shared the middle tier with Marlon. Above them were Tito and Jermaine, beneath them was Jackie. The girls slept in the living room. Becoming accustomed to living in such a crowded environment was good experience for the boys, who would before long be touring the world and therefore living in each others' pockets on the road. It might have been a humble home but it was, neighbours recall, kept spotless by Katherine. She also promoted religious values in the house, having become a Jehovah's Witness when Michael turned five. He would follow his mother into the religion, which meant – among many other things – that he would not celebrate birthdays or Christmas.

These were tough times emotionally for Michael, not least due to Joseph's volatile nature, the results of which have been widely documented. Joseph regularly physically disciplined his sons and these instances sometimes spilled over into something beyond discipline. He would routinely push the boys against walls and trip them up, as well as beating them. He smacked Michael when he was just three years old. Furiously upset, the youngster threw a shoe at his father in protest. Joseph told his son he had signed his own death warrant and beat him so badly that Katherine intervened, fearful for her son's life. At last, Michael was released from his father's grip. He ran away, screaming at his father that he hated him. For this, he received a fresh beating. Katherine had long been concerned and terrified by Joseph's behaviour towards his sons. He had once – and once only – struck his wife, soon after the birth of their first child. Katherine's response was immediate: she threw a ceramic object at him, drawing blood where it landed, and warned him to never hit her again if he did not want to lose her. He never harmed her again, physically at least.

Instead, he turned his considerable wrath onto his sons. Other 'punishments' meted out to them by Joseph included locking Michael in a cupboard, and there were cruel mental games too. He once tripped his son up and told him that he had done so in response to something Michael had done the previous day. He then added: 'Tomorrow I'm gonna get you for what you do today.' Michael protested that he had done nothing wrong yet today. 'Oh, you will,' said his father. He also mocked his son about his appearance. Later, to teach his children not to leave their windows open in the evening, Joseph jumped through an open window into their bedroom and screamed noisily at them while wearing a frightening mask. For years after, young Michael had nightmares about being kidnapped from his bed. All of this left Michael increasingly wary of his father. He did his best to avoid him around the house and would feel sick – sometimes to the point of vomiting – when he encountered or thought of his father.

'He was very strict, very hard,' he told Oprah Winfrey in 1993. 'Just a look would scare you. There have been times when he'd come to see me and I'd get sick, start to throw up.' In a subsequent television interview, Joseph responded to Michael's account of his childhood. 'I whipped him with a switch and belt. I never beat him,' he insisted. 'You beat someone with a stick.' He also insisted that his treatment of Michael had moulded him into 'one of the best artists in the world'. Tito gave some credence to this claim when he said that Michael's fine dance moves had originated from his desperate dodging of his father's fists. Perhaps the simmering undercurrent of fury that was seen in many of Michael's moves could also be thus explained. All the same, the legacy of Joseph's behaviour will surely have been enormously negative on all the children, and has been the cause of much speculation in Michael's case particularly.

Katherine worked in a department store and Joseph had rarely been short of work, but little of it was either high-paying or inspiring. He had taken jobs as a crane operator, a welder and a crop harvester. The hours were often long, the pay invariably modest – it was fortunate that Joseph, like Katherine, had a strong work ethic. All the same, he felt restless and wanted more out of life. He believed in the American dream and, this being the 1960s, his mind turned to the music industry as a way of realizing it. Together with his brother Luther and five friends he formed a rock band called The Falcons which performed in clubs, bars and other venues, bringing some much-needed excitement and extra funds to the household. Joseph played guitar and his three eldest sons would often sit and watch as the band rehearsed the songs of Otis Redding and Chuck Berry.

The Falcons were not successful enough to last long. They soon gave up on their dream and Joseph moodily put away his guitar in his bedroom cupboard. It was a symbolic moment: he was attempting to forget that he had ever aimed for something more than life in dreary, hardworking industries. The guitar – and with it the dream – was not to stay hidden for long, though. Katherine occasionally took it out and played songs for her children. The boys themselves sometimes secretly played the guitar, too, when Joseph – who had forbidden them to touch the instrument – was at work. Their mother soon became aware of these sessions after walking in on one, but mindful of the likely outcome of Joseph learning of them, she did not tell her husband. She had always been a generous woman who encouraged her children's interests. 'If I developed an interest in movie stars, for instance,' Michael wrote in *Moonwalk*, 'she'd come home with an armful of books about famous stars. Even with nine children she treated each of us like an only child.'

So with Katherine turning a blind eye, the musical sessions around Joseph's abandoned guitar continued. When Tito – who was proving a promising musician, having started to learn saxophone at school – accidentally snapped one of the instrument's strings, he feared a beating from his father when he realized what had been going on while his back was turned. Tito's worries proved upsettingly correct: Joseph screamed at and beat Tito. However, in the aftermath of that storm, his father calmed down and agreed to hear Tito play the guitar. As the boy strummed chords, his brothers Jermaine and Jackie provided some sparse vocal accompaniments. It was the first time they performed in front of an 'audience'. Joseph was shocked by how well his sons performed. His dreams of music industry success were re-ignited in that moment – he simply transferred his aspirations to his sons.

When he returned from work some nights later his mood could not have been more contrasting to when he had discovered the broken string. He appeared with a huge, beaming smile and proudly presented Tito with his own instrument, a red electric guitar. He then put his three eldest sons through their first rehearsal while Michael and Marlon looked on, wide-eyed, from the side. Music was indeed proving a healing force in the Jackson household, at least temporarily: the family had never been closer or happier. 'We had found something special,' said Tito later. Before this, the family had been closest when they assembled in front of the oven on cold winter days, desperately seeking heat. These musical rehearsals became a daily affair, lasting for several hours each time. 'I really went to work with them,' Joseph told *Time* magazine.

There was lots of crime in Gary in those days. Joseph and Katherine were concerned for their children's safety and preferred them not to play in the street with other youths. With the new musical venture underway, the boys spent even more of their spare time within the walls of the family home. This provoked considerable suspicion and resentment from other residents of the neighbourhood, who mistook their behaviour as prompted by a sense of aloof superiority rather than the combination of security and ambition which actually underlined it. Taunts would be aimed at the Jackson family and rocks were sometimes thrown at the house. Michael saw this as a test from God. Meanwhile, at home, the Jackson boys were still facing the brutality of their father. Driven by his oft-stated belief that there are only two types of people in the world – winners and losers – his obsession that none of his children would be in the latter camp led him to explosive moments during rehearsals. Joseph would sit threateningly brandishing a belt and he attacked any band member who messed up.

Under Joseph's watchful eye, the practising continued. Marlon soon joined the line-up. He had little discernible musical talent but was a promising dancer and his mother was insistent that he be allowed to join. He was five years old. Michael, one year Marlon's junior, was still a mere spectator at this stage. That changed one day when he copied Jermaine's vocal rendition of a James Brown song. Michael had long copied things his older brother did in day to day life, and was also customarily clothed in Jermaine's hand-me-downs. When he mimicked Jermaine's vocals, his voice was so beautiful and powerful that Katherine was instantly mesmerized. She could not wait to tell Joseph of her discovery. Joseph has said he hopes his boys' musical talent was inherited from him but much credit can also be given to Katherine for the musical talent in the family. Prior to her quiet approval of their furtive guitar sessions, when their television set had broken in 1955 she had gathered her children for a sing-a-long. Indeed, there was a history of fine vocals on her side of the family. Her great-grandfather, former Alabaman slave Kendall Brown, was a regular singer at his local church and had a widely celebrated voice. Michael believed that he inherited his voice from his mother 'and God', though Katherine brushes this off, saying she does not know where his talent came from. With his addition to the line-up, the band had a new vocal talent and a nascent version of the Jackson Five was complete. In his autobiography *Moonwalk*, Michael was keen to stress that he felt no pressure to join the band and pursue fame. 'I wasn't *forced* into this business by stage parents the way Judy Garland was,' he wrote. 'I did it because I enjoyed it and because it was as natural to me as drawing breath and exhaling it. I did it because I was compelled to do it, not by parents or family, but by my own inner life in the world of music.' Soon he was sent to school. He initially hated kindergarten and was traumatized when his mother left him there on his first day. He then moved to the Garnett Elementary School, where he grew to love education and became something of a teacher's pet. He would sometimes secretly take items of Katherine's jewellery collection to give to his favourite tutors as gifts.

At Garnett, he gave what was perhaps his first ever public solo performance. He sang the show tune 'Climb Ev'ry Mountain' from the musical *The Sound of Music*, which had been in existence only four years at this stage. It was an amazing, a cappella performance that mesmerized Michael's classmates and teacher alike. The children gave him a standing ovation and the teacher burst into tears. 'I had made them happy,' Michael later remembered fondly. His ability had been noted at home, too. When she had first heard him copy Jermaine's rendition of the James Brown tune, Katherine had believed that he should become the band's lead vocalist. Jackie, too, saw Michael as the natural leader for the band onstage. Jermaine was hurt but complied with the request that he be replaced at the front by his younger brother.

The Jackson brothers had their line-up complete and their act finely honed, thanks to their dedication and their father's (at times unpleasant) focused tutoring. They began to enter talent shows and nearly always returned home with the trophy in their hands. One time, Michael remembered, having passed the award between the brothers, they propped it up on the front seat of the car, as if it were a baby. Michael's talent and showmanship was key to their successes – during a performance of the song 'Barefootin'' at one talent contest he dramatically kicked off his shoes and danced barefooted. Soon, the small Jackson household was filling up with such silverware. The family was poor and Joseph's rage continued to cast a shadow, but all the same Michael recalled these days as happy ones. His parents were delighted with their sons' success and the disruptive influences of money, contracts and commercial pressure were yet to cast a shadow.

Neighbours, too, remembered these times. 'Me and my mother used to go over to their house and we used to watch them practise,'

Jerry Macon told *The Times*. 'I remember when they first started practising, [Michael] used to play the bongos. They would be playing a song and he would be playing the bongos and he would put them down and get up and dance. He was about five years old. He wasn't dancing like he was dancing later, but he was a good dancer. That was before he even started singing.' Macon's mother recalls Michael as a well-behaved lad. 'Michael was a great little boy, somewhat shy,' she said. 'He would not talk that much, only when you talked to him. He always had a good voice, but I did not think too much of it. I did not ever think they would become famous.'

Joseph, though, was convinced that his sons were destined for the top and must fulfil that promise. As a result of his ambition, he began to plan for what he was convinced would be a glittering future for them. Joseph was sure of his sons' potential and consequently invested heavily in instruments and other musical equipment for the band. Katherine was terrified by what she saw as his reckless spending and urged him to stop. Joseph did not heed her pleas, so convinced was he of his sons' talent. He also took to spending entire weekends away from home, watching other bands perform live and learning as much as he could about the music industry. Amid the criticism of him for the way he 'disciplined' his boys, it is worth noting that it was his unshakeable belief in their talent that propelled them to fame. In none of his sons did he have more belief than in Michael.

This often led to Michael being singled out by his father, he claimed. When his brothers failed to live up to Michael's brilliance, Joseph would shout at them to 'Do it like Michael'. This naturally led to sibling resentment brewing in the band. As time went on, their father's fury increased. Ruling the band with an iron fist, he punished Michael for unpunctuality by pushing him into a drum kit. Michael was also whipped with a belt and with the electrical flex from a fridge. Michael was shaken and upset by this, but credits his father with making the band what they were. He says that although he was a 'horrible man', he was an amazing manager. He often spoke of his father in such a dichotomy. 'My father was a management genius,' he told the Oxford Union in 2001, 'but what I really wanted was a dad.' He found that an effective – if short-term – way of getting his father to stop his assaults was to threaten to never sing again.

The management genius side of Joseph's mixed personality had quickly honed the band into a unit ready to perform live at more than just talent shows. It was time for their first paid shows. Proud Joseph and the boys would squeeze into their Volkswagen van and take to the road in pursuit of fame and fortune. Michael, just eight years old, was the lead vocalist and front man. Tito played guitar, Jermaine was the bassist, Jackie played maracas and Marlon provided backing vocals and dancing. Meanwhile, two non-family members had joined: the coincidentally-surnamed Johnny Jackson played drums and Ronny Rancifer was on the keyboards. (Motown, in a PR spin, would later claim that the duo were cousins of the Jackson brothers.) They quickly became a tight unit and changed their name from The Jackson Brothers to the more snappy Jackson Five, at the suggestion of a lady who had watched them perform at a department store. (They had for a while also gone under the extraordinarily unwieldy name of The Ripple and Waves Plus Michael.)

Their first paid performance was at a Gary nightclub called Mr Lucky's, where their fee was a modest $7. In subsequent performances the band would be showered by notes and coins from the audience. Michael would hastily collect the money and used it to buy bagfuls of confectionary for him and his brothers to enjoy as they travelled round. The sweets would help get them through a hectic weekend of performing, before the reality of school dawned on Monday morning. Having initially confined their shows to venues relatively near to Gary, The Jackson Five then moved to larger venues, with audiences running into thousands. They played numerous cities including Boston, Cleveland and Philadelphia. At these larger venues they often shared the bill with well-known acts such as James Brown, The Temptations and The Four Tops. Michael and his brothers were very much on the rise – what youngster would not have been excited by such fame and glamour?

All the same, for Michael something was missing. Looking back on this period in 1993, he told Oprah Winfrey: 'I remember going to the recording studio and there was a park across the street and I'd see all the children playing and I would cry because it would make me sad that I would have to work instead.' It was during live performances, he said, that he felt he truly came alive. 'I was most comfortable on stage,' he said, sounding every inch the consummate showman. 'Once I got off stage, I was very sad. Lonely and sad. There were times when I had great times with my brothers, but I used to cry from loneliness. You don't get to do things that other children get to do. It was always work, work, work. One concert to the next. The recording studio. Television shows. Photo sessions. Always something to do. I didn't have friends.'

True, the band was commanding the attention of larger venues at times, but some of the venues chosen for them were less prestigious. The band played in strip clubs and there the nine-year-old Michael was confronted with a bawdy atmosphere. Backstage the brothers would sometimes discover peepholes that granted them views of women bathing and changing. He was also confronted with the realities of his father's infidelities. Joseph would often pick up groupies and openly take them into his hotel room. Michael and his brothers were forced to listen to the resulting activities from their own room. He was disgusted by what he heard, and felt terrible that he was forced to deceive his mother by not revealing to her what went on during the tours.

Having already faced jibes from his father for his 'ugliness', Michael then had to deal with more comments about his appearance from other performers on the live circuit. More than one responded to the fact that the lead singer of the Jackson Five was also the shortest member by making quips about his size, accusing him of being a 'midget'. Joseph told Michael to get used to such comments, but Michael was inconsolable. 'I don't like it,' he said. 'They're talking bad about me.' Interestingly, for a man who in adulthood would be compared to a child, as a youngster Michael was considered older than his years. 'They called me a forty-two-year-old midget,' he later said in an ITV documentary. He was puzzled by this, and also began to tire of being the cute one of the band. 'I like all our fans,' he says in *Michael Jackson: The Visual Documentary*, 'even the ones who keep calling me "cute". But I'm getting bigger every day so they'll have to call me something else.' Later, he looked back on this period during an interview with

Oprah Winfrey. Michael told her he felt 'lonely, sad, having to face popularity and all that. There were times when I had great times with my brothers, pillow fights and things, but I…used to always cry from loneliness.'

He responded to that loneliness by becoming ever more focused on success. Michael's thorough nature soon came to the surface. He routinely remained in the wings after a band performance, so he could study the shows of other acts. It was not just their dance moves he memorized, it was the entire performance and all it entailed including, he recalled, the 'emotion' of it. 'The greatest education in the world is watching the masters at work,' he wrote. 'You couldn't teach a person what I've learned just standing and watching.' On one occasion, he distracted a performer he was watching, so intently was he staring at her. He later apologized backstage and she was so charmed by young Michael that she taught him a few onstage moves. His exhaustiveness showed again when they played the Apollo Theater in Harlem. There they were shown a section of the 'Tree of Hope' which stood backstage. The tree had become a musical legend thanks to its associations with a Louis Armstrong performance, and it was believed that touching it prior to taking the stage would bring good luck to the performer. Each of the brothers duly touched the log. Michael, though, returned to the log to touch it a second time. They duly put in a winning performance on the night, and the relative fortunes subsequently enjoyed by Michael over his brothers will have left him feeling his superstitious return to the Tree of Hope was vindicated.

* * *

These were astonishingly exciting times for Michael and his brothers. They were moving up in stature on the live circuit. After earning just $7 for their first live performance, they were soon commanding fees closer to $700. Their ultimate dreams of a record deal and true fame were becoming more attainable all the time. Their first record contract came when Michael was just nine, in 1967, with Steeltown Records, which as its name suggests was a local label. Having been at school from Monday to Friday, the boys and Joseph would arrive at the label's studios on Saturday mornings for recording sessions. True, Steeltown was not a large label by any standards, but this did not diminish their excitement. The first song to emerge commercially from these sessions was the single 'Big Boy', which was released in January 1968. Written by Ed Silver, the song's chorus heard Michael boast that he was 'a big boy now'. It premiered on American radio station WWCA and was mainly sold by the band themselves at their live performances. The second single the band released through Steeltown had a similar theme and was called 'We Don't Have to Be Over 21 (to Fall in Love)'. Neither song was particularly memorable and neither charted. However, for the band there was joyful pride in how far they had already come. Michael recalled with a smile the time the family sat round the radio in their living room and heard 'Big Boy' broadcast live. At the conclusion of the song, the Jacksons' personal tensions were all forgotten as the family laughed with excitement and the brothers and their mother hugged each other. Joseph generally shied away from such physical affection.

Michael again showed his focused, precocious side when the band assembled for a publicity photograph three months after the release of 'Big Boy'. He complained that the way they were lined up was going to make the photograph look more like a standard family shot, rather than a picture of a band. Challenged by Joseph to correct the positioning, Michael did just that. He moved his brothers round and then took his place kneeling down in front of them. Steeltown executive Ben Brown, quoted in *Michael Jackson: The Magic and the Madness*, recalled how impressed he was by the nine-year-old's vision. 'That was a great shot,' he said. 'How did he know how to do that, how to take a publicity photo? He was such an old soul, as if he had been a superstar in another life.'

The Jackson Five soon moved to a new label – the legendary Motown Records. Founded by Berry Gordy in 1959 – when Michael had yet to celebrate his first birthday – it launched the careers of many of the most celebrated black artists of the twentieth century, including Stevie Wonder, Marvin Gaye, The Supremes and The Temptations. By 1968 it was a successful and influential label which had created its own genre: the Motown Sound. The Jackson Five had already sent a demo tape to the label's president, Berry Gordy, when singer Gladys Knight invited some Motown representatives to watch the band perform at the Regal Theater in Chicago. The breakthrough came months later when another singer, Bobby Taylor, also contacted Motown about the band having seen them perform. They were invited to audition at the Saunders Building in Detroit – the then home of Motown Records. Michael – a keen fan of the board game Monopoly – compared the journey to the label's headquarters as akin to the conclusion of that game. He hoped they would win. They drove off with sandwiches made by their mother and eventually arrived in Detroit. They stayed at the Gotham Hotel, which the label had booked for them, and had an early night. The next morning, they arrived at the Motown building on 2648 West Grand Boulevard, pulling up in the trusty Volkswagen van. Purchased by Gordy in 1958, the building had been renamed Hitsville USA to underline the ambitions of the label. Michael, though, was nonplussed. 'It looked kind of run down,' he was to remember. As the brothers nervously eyed the famous structure, Joseph made them line up on the pavement and gave them a pep talk, ordering them to behave themselves. The band and its father then presented themselves at reception.

Having been flattered when the first Motown employee to greet them knew who each of them was, the Jacksons were disappointed when they learned that president Gordy was not to be present at the audition as he was in Los Angeles. Instead, they were joined in the studio by ten Motown employees, including Gordy's creative assistant Suzanne dePasse and vice president Ralph Seltzer. The band would perform on a small wooden stage in front of the staff members and the audition would be filmed and sent to Gordy for his comments. 'Then,' said Seltzer, the president would 'render a decision'. Joseph initially insisted that the band return on a day when Gordy was present, but eventually agreed that the audition would go ahead as planned.

Once the band and their equipment were assembled onstage, it was time to start the audition. Michael took the lead, announcing that the first song they were to sing was 'I Got the Feeling' by James Brown. With Joseph watching, arms folded, and dePasse and Seltzer smiling approvingly, the band put in a great perform-ance. Michael was particularly mesmerizing, singing with a soulfulness beyond his years and dancing so well that Brown himself would have been proud of the youngster. All the same, it was an unnatural environment for the band to perform in. There was no applause or comments from their audience between the songs. Before the second song, Michael introduced each band member in turn and they then performed 'Tobacco Road'. The third and final track from the band was 'Who's Lovin' You' by Smokey Robinson. Michael was so unnerved by the silence which greeted the conclusion of the set that he boyishly asked the room: 'How was that?' His older brother Jermaine told him to be quiet. Seltzer calmly stood up, thanked the Jacksons for coming and sent the band back to the Gotham Hotel to await their decision. He told them to expect it in two days' time, once Gordy had viewed the film.

On seeing the footage of the audition, the president was immedi-ately impressed by the band – particularly Michael himself. 'When I first heard him sing Smokey's song, "Who's Lovin' You", at ten years old, it felt like he had lived the song for fifty years,' remembered Gordy. 'Somehow, even at that first meeting with him, he had a hunger to learn, a hunger to be the best and was willing to work as hard and as long as it took.' One of the Motowners present at the audition was producer Hank Crosby, whose wife Pat told the *Detroit Free Press* of the excitement Michael and his brothers sparked in her husband. 'I can recall the look in his eyes when he came home and told me about the audition,' she said. 'He was absolutely blown out the water, just amazed. I've always remembered his exact words: "I have no doubt that these kids are going to cover the world."' Gordy agreed and instantly instructed that the band be signed to Motown. 'Don't waste a second – sign them!' he ordered his colleagues.

The family were summoned back to the Motown headquarters where Joseph was presented with the contracts. Seltzer, who conducted the negotiations for Motown, told Joseph that his sons were going to be 'Big, big, *big*'. He then explained that the label was suggesting a term of seven years for the deal. Joseph insisted that this was too long, and demanded that the deal be for no longer than one year. After some calls to Gordy, it was agreed to reduce the length of the commitment to Joseph's preferred one year. It was only later that he realized his victory was a hollow one: the contract stipulated that for five years after the termination of the deal the band would be prevented from recording with any other label. This was not to be the only clause that would provoke conflict and litigation in the future.

Meanwhile, the boys waited outside in the corridor. Although their father's negotiations with Seltzer went on for some hours, they did not misbehave. 'They were extremely well-mannered,' recalled Seltzer. 'People would come in and say, "Ralph, who are those kids out in the hall? They don't run up and down, or bother anybody, or wrestle with each other. They're just sitting there being good."' How much of this behaviour was a result of Joseph's iron fist is hard to say. Finally, with the meeting over, Joseph called his boys into the office. With a wide grin, he told them that they had a deal with Motown. The family hugged each other and some of the boys jumped for joy. Each boy then signed the contract –

without having read it – and Joseph duly put his name on the parental consent contract. 'Congratulations,' said Seltzer. 'May I be the first to welcome you to Motown Records!' It was 26 July 1968, and Michael Jackson's inked signature was drying on his contract with Motown Records.

* * *

Soon, the first part of the band's myth was being created. It was put about that the band had been discovered by none other than Motown star Diana Ross. She first saw them, so the story went, at a concert at the Gilroy Stadium in Gary in September 1968. Having been impressed by their performance she contacted Gordy and urged him to sign them. The truth, of course, was that the band had already been signed to Motown for two months when this concert took place. Furthermore, Ross had not even been in the audience at the Gilroy Stadium. The Ross story had been concocted by the then chief of publicity at Motown, Mike Roshkind. 'He thought it was very good, PR-wise,' recalled Seltzer. 'How exciting is "Bobby Taylor told Ralph Seltzer, who set up a Saturday audition"? But "Diana Ross saw this group and thought they were fantastic"? That's exciting.' The band duly met Ross in December at a party at Gordy's extravagant Detroit mansion, where Michael was astonished by the scale and plushness of the home. She was particularly taken with Michael. 'You're just so cute,' she told him, squeezing his cheek. Just as Ross was taken with Michael, so was his father enamoured of Ross. It was to prove an upsetting experience for Katherine when she was eventually introduced to the woman who had become a maternal figure for her son and an object of lust for her husband. Katherine felt unattractive when compared to Ross and the contrast was exacerbated by her limp, the legacy of a childhood bout of polio. 'Michael needs his mother,' Katherine would say to Ross, who quickly disappeared in a flustered state.

Ross discovering The Jackson Five was not the only fabrication spun around the band in the early days. Although he was ten at this point, Michael was presented to the media as an eight-year-old. At first he was confused by this discrepancy, but he quickly learned the fine art of public relations. When the band was presented to the press in Beverly Hills on 11 August 1969, he was asked how it felt to be a star. 'Well, to tell you the truth,' he smiled, 'I had just about given up hope!' When the same journalist suspiciously pressed him about his age, he remained steadfast and smiling. The matter was soon diffused. (Given Ross's presumed compliance in the spin, it is not without irony that, in her sleeve notes for The Jackson Five's debut album, she wrote: 'Honesty has always been a very special word for me – a special idea.') Michael's savvy way with the media was admirable.

Once the band had signed with Motown, Michael continued to stand out from the pack in his performances too. 'Michael was a born star,' enthused Gordy in the *Mirror*. 'He was a classic example of understanding everything. I recognized that he had a depth that was so vast, it was just incredible. The first time I saw him, I saw this little kid as something special.' However, the early months of the band's relationship with Motown were not promising. The band recorded a host of songs at the label's recording studios in Detroit but none were released. Motown had to pay a fee to

Steeltown to gain full control of the band and before long the various costs of The Jackson Five were running into tens of thousands of dollars.

The band and Joseph were moved to Hollywood, and worked hard in the studio. Michael was entranced by the Tinseltown culture: the fast cars, the glamorous people, the lines of palm trees. 'It was like being in another country,' he wrote in *Moonwalk*. 'I was uncontrollable...Disneyland, Sunset Strip, the beach. Every day was special.' In the studio they worked on a track called 'I Wanna Be Free'. Deke Richards, who had co-written the track, worked with the band in the studio. He found no lack of willingness to work hard from the brothers, but needed to hone Michael's vocal delivery. As for Michael, he was surprized by what a lengthy process it was to record a song. The song itself – re-titled 'I Want You Back' – was recorded more than twenty times before the producers were happy with it. Finally, at two in the morning, after Michael had nearly fallen asleep at the microphone, the song was complete. It had not just been a lengthy process, but an expensive one too, costing five times what a normal Motown single would cost to produce in those days.

'I Want You Back' was released in October 1969. After a modest start – it debuted at number ninety in the Billboard Top 100 – it eventually went to number one, after some hard work by the label's promotion team paid off. It was promoted on television shows including *Hollywood Palace Special*, where additional string parts backed the standard tune. The band had their first number-one hit, and the song did well elsewhere, too, reaching number two in the United Kingdom. It ultimately sold more than 6 million copies worldwide. It was the first international hit for The Jackson 5, the latest name and phrasing of the band. The band had almost been given a different name which would have reflected the fact that, more and more, Michael was standing out from the pack. As revealed in Taraborrelli's book, Gordy and Deke toyed with the idea of calling the band The Jackson Five Featuring Michael Jackson. Likewise, when they made their first national television appearance, their introduction by Diana Ross focused on one member. 'Tonight, I have the pleasure of introducing a young star who has been in the business all of his life. He's worked with his family, and when he sings and dances, he lights up the stage.' She then introduced 'Michael Jackson and The Jackson Five'. Joseph was furious at the way one son had been singled out, but Ross – with whom Michael was by this point living – was unrepentant. (Later, when Tito got engaged, Gordy underscored Michael's importance by saying he had no objection to any of the brothers marrying – apart from Michael.)

The focus was on Ross once more in the title of the band's debut album: *Diana Ross Presents The Jackson 5*, which was released in December 1969. Alongside 'I Want You Back' were tracks including the Disney classic 'Zip-a-Dee-Doo-Dah', and covers of the recently released Stevie Wonder track 'My Cherie Amour' and the Sly Stone song 'Stand'. It sold over 600,000 copies and received some promising critical reviews. 'It combines some authentically good songs with the inevitable Motown blueprint specials,' said *Rolling Stone* magazine, adding: 'Given any kind of decent material at all, The Jackson 5 should be able to give…many years of good, tight music.' They were soon on the front cover of *Soul* magazine. A number-one hit, critical praise – Michael and his brothers were very much on their way.

The band's next release was the single 'ABC', a catchy track with a similar chord-structure to their debut. It was, Michael said later, one of the favourite tracks he recorded for Motown. Released on 24 February 1970, it reached number one in America – knocking The Beatles' 'Let It Be' off the top spot – and number eight in Britain. With their success growing, The Jackson 5 released their third single just twelve weeks later. 'The Love You Save' also had musical similarities to the first two singles: a brand was clearly being created. Again, it knocked The Beatles off the number-one spot in America; this time the Fab Four's 'The Long and Winding Road' was the victim. Successful times for Michael, but they came at a price, as he told Winfrey in 1993. 'Well, you don't get to do things that other children get to do, having friends and slumber parties and buddies,' he explained to her. 'There was none of that for me. I didn't have friends when I was little. My brothers were my friends.' He did, though, have the honour, along with his brothers, of singing the American national anthem at the opening of the baseball World Series at Riverfront Stadium in Ohio. They released the festive double-A side 'Santa Claus Is Coming to Town'/'Christmas Won't Be the Same This Year' in November 1970.

* * *

With their growing success in the charts around the world, Michael and his brothers were soon faced by ever more hysterical behaviour from their fans. They were mobbed by thousands at airports and concerts, with Michael having to beg the audience to leave the stage at one event. Frequently, they would have to leave the venue before the closing track was over and rush into waiting cars which would whisk them away before the audience knew they had left. 'I don't know if I can do this,' whimpered a terrified Michael after one public mobbing. 'Maybe for a little while, but not for ever.' Although he was learning some of the pitfalls of fame, he still remained naïve about much of what was to come for him. For instance, when Ross warned him that celebrities could get hurt by the fame game, he did not believe her. 'I don't see how,' he shrugged. He soon learned, when in November 1970, a scheduled concert in Buffalo, New York, had to be called off after death threats were made against him. A security officer would be appointed for the next tour. The same month, three gigs in Texas were also cancelled when the Southern Christian Leadership Council's Operation Breadbasket protested that a white promoter should not be working on the dates.

There was a happier moment for Michael and his family when they journeyed back to Gary by helicopter, receiving the key to the city. They were greeted by thousands of proud locals, including former classmates of the brothers. They put on a performance for the people of Gary. 'The children really enjoyed that show,' Garnett Elementary School head teacher Gladys Johnson recalled in *Time* magazine. 'I could not believe how they idolized those Jackson 5 boys.' As for Michael's education, it was being increasingly disrupted by fame. The demands of his musical career meant he could only sporadically attend classes and when a death threat was issued against him, he was hastily withdrawn and educated at home. This took him even further away from normality. He spent much of his life at this time in hotels, and he took to using the freight lifts rather than the public ones. The reason? To avoid 'normal people'. It was scenes such as those which greeted the band on arrival in London that had helped turn the youngster's head. At Heathrow Airport they were engulfed by a mob of screaming girls. Michael lost one of his shoes and was almost asphyxiated when two female fans grabbed an end of his scarf each. Later in their visit to England the police were forced to use water hoses to disperse Jackson 5 fans who had arrived at their hotel, one of them threatening an employee with a knife unless she was allowed access to Michael's room. Another time, a girl was – according to a story Michael told – cut across the throat by broken glass when a herd of fans broke a record shop window while trying to get the chance to touch him.

Amid the Jacksonmania their UK tour was a success. A reviewer from *The Times* attended the band's concert at the Liverpool Empire. 'Fourteen-year-old Michael has an astonishing command of gesture and his twinkling feet scarcely seemed to touch the stage,' read the subsequent write-up. His family were quick to insist that the way in which Michael was being singled out for praise would not go to his head. 'Michael is pretty stable,' his mother insisted in an interview with *Time* magazine. 'I think it's his raisin'. We used to talk to the boys about getting big heads. None of them is better than anyone else. One might have a little more talent, but that doesn't make you better.' Try telling that to their army of young fans, who screamed loudest for Michael.

Some of the brothers were happy to take advantage of all this female attention. So too was Joseph, who was not averse to picking up groupies himself. Michael, however, was appalled by this tendency. Not only did he not indulge in sex with fans, he would also warn them not to sleep with his 'mean' brothers. When he encountered one fan who had just slept with Jackie, he was shocked to discover she did so voluntarily. 'Why would you *want* to?' he asked, revolted and puzzled. Having been forced to listen to his father's sex sessions through hotel walls, he was now even closer to the action, often having to pretend to be asleep as Jermaine brought girls to the hotel room they shared. Soon after this, when Katherine threatened to divorce Joseph, Michael complained to Ross that his father was a 'bad man' and that his brothers were 'going down the same road'. In his autobiography and then again during a television interview in 2003, Michael stated that his first girlfriend was Tatum O'Neal, the actress daughter of Ryan O'Neal. He claims that O'Neal 'came on' to him. O'Neal disputes she ever had a relationship with him, though confirmed they did kiss briefly in 1982. She told the *Mirror*: 'He was a huge star but it seemed he barely even dated and knew little about life. He once came to my house and asked to come upstairs because he'd never been in a girl's bedroom before. He sat on the bed and we kissed very briefly, but it was all very awkward.'

O'Neal's account of Michael's inexperience in the early 1980s is corroborated by singer Stephanie Mills, who says she had a romance of sorts with Michael in the late 1970s while he was filming *The Wiz*. 'I thought I was going to marry Michael,' she told a radio interviewer. 'We never had sex, I never had sex with

Michael.' That said, she described him as 'very much a man, very loving and caring' and added that 'he's a great kisser'. Mills claims she was the only black woman Michael ever dated.

* * *

In September 1971 the ABC television network began to air a Saturday morning cartoon called *The Jackson 5ive*. It was to run for two seasons. Soon more Jackson 5 singles followed, including 'Never Can Say Goodbye' (which sold an estimated 1.6 million copies in America) and 'Maybe Tomorrow' (originally written for Sammy Davis Jr). However, Motown soon began to release Michael's solo records to follow the example set by Donny Osmond, who was enjoying solo success while still a member of The Osmond Brothers. The first solo Michael Jackson single was 'Got To Be There', released in October 1971. With this release he became the label's first artist to 'go solo' while still a member of a group. In little over a year, two more solo singles had been released. The first was 'Rockin' Robin', which reached number two in the American charts. It had not originally been intended as a single, until radio disc jockeys seized on it. Then came 'Ben', his first solo number one. In this song, originally intended for Donny Osmond, he sang of his friendship with a rat. It was an eccentric subject for a song, but would in retrospect be perfectly fitting for Michael, who went on to become obsessed with animals and who would pursue plenty of peculiar associations. Initially the sleeve of the record included images of rats, but this was changed after complaints from frightened fans. It went on to sell 1.7 million copies in America alone.

While he was reaping the rewards from his solo releases, the chart fortunes of The Jackson 5 were in decline and so was their relationship with Motown. Joseph had arranged for the band to perform a series of shows in Las Vegas – it was there that Michael first met his future wife, Lisa Marie Presley – and had done so against the advice of Gordy, who was convinced the venture would be a failure. However, when the residency proved a roaring success, Gordy issued a press release effectively claiming credit for the idea. Joseph was furious. Relations between band and label were falling apart, and even a secret meeting Michael had with Gordy failed to save the relationship. The band voted to leave Motown and were quickly signed – minus Jermaine, who remained at Motown, having married Berry Gordy's daughter Hazel – to the Epic division of CBS Records in June 1975. Jermaine was replaced by Michael's younger brother Randy. At their new label, they hoped for a fresh start. They certainly needed a fresh name, after Motown enforced its contractual right to retain the name The Jackson 5.

After waiting for the terms of their Motown contract to expire, the newly renamed band – The Jacksons – released their first CBS album. It included a song written by Michael – 'Blues Away', which was co-produced by the band. They were very much enjoying the creative involvement which their new label allowed them to have. Another track on the album, 'Enjoy Yourself', was released as their first CBS single and gave them a number-six hit – their finest showing for three years. It reached number forty-two in the UK. Meanwhile, Jermaine faced the embarrassment of his debut solo record for Motown reaching only number 164. Michael was disgusted when his father failed to show any sympathy for their brother's misfortune. Soon, their own releases were also performing disappointingly. Their second album reached no higher than number sixty-three. However, Michael was about to embark on a project that would resurrect his fame and appeal.

CHAPTER TWO

I n 1977, Michael met Queen Elizabeth II. The royal appointment came in May when he and the band undertook a three-week European tour. He met Her Majesty after The Jacksons left the stage at the Royal Command Performance in Glasgow to honour her Silver Jubilee. He was to recall the evening fondly. 'When I actually looked into the Queen's eyes,' he said, 'it was the greatest thing.' However, the most epochal moment of his career to date came in July, when he was to meet the person who truly had the greatest impact on his life.

* * *

Michael always enjoyed musical theatre and he had been most taken by the 1975 all-black Broadway production of *The Wiz* – based on the L. Frank Baum novel *The Wonderful Wizard of Oz*. He had loved the performances, but little could he have known then that he would star in a film of the play in 1978, nor how that experience would alter his musical career and life so drastically. As soon as Rob Cohen of Motown Productions decided to embark on a cinematic version of the play, he cast Diana Ross in the all-important role of

Dorothy. Michael was then approached to play the role of the Scarecrow and – despite initial concern from Joseph – accepted the offer. He moved to Manhattan for the filming, with sister LaToya accompanying him as a surrogate mother figure in the Big Apple.

It was hard work for Michael. Cast and crew worked six days a week and he routinely had to rise as early as 4 a.m. to allow time to get into his role. However, he loved the city that never sleeps and adored the heavy make-up he had to wear for the part. His father's jibes about his appearance must have seemed a distant memory. He also related to his character, who he saw as a misunderstood outsider in an at times unforgiving world. During his rare time off, he played around in the thirty-seventh-floor apartment that he and LaToya shared. On one occasion, a visitor recalled, he playfully draped himself over the edge of the balcony and pretended he was going to jump to his death. There would be a high-profile reprise of this moment later in Michael's life. He was also taken to hospital one day after a trip to Coney Island ended abruptly when he collapsed with chest pains and shortness of breath. Another incident from this era, at the home of director Sidney Lumet, revealed that Michael – a young man who had performed on stage in front of thousands – still suffered from nerves. Some friends of Lumet's teenage daughter asked Michael to sing for them one evening. Michael agreed, but only if everyone in the room would cover their eyes as he sang. 'I think he was embarrassed by the closeness of the situation,' Lumet told *Time* magazine, 'but his desire not to be rude or to hurt her [Lumet's daughter] led him to say yes.'

Gossip journalist Liz Smith, writing on the 'Women on the Web' internet site, recalled meeting Michael on the set of *The*

Wiz. 'There was nothing, and I mean nothing, to suggest what was to come, in terms of eccentricity,' she wrote. 'He had yet to alter his face at all. He was a handsome young man. The vibe he put out was one of eager, honest, hardworking drive.' Indeed, he was so focused on getting his part right that he took to studying television footage showing the movements of gazelles, cheetahs and panthers in order to perfect the sort of body language required for the part. This was effort well-spent: *The Wiz* was a commercial and critical flop on its release, but Michael's contribution was one of the few things positively mentioned by reviewers and audiences alike.

One member of the crew watched Michael with particular admiration. During filming, Michael comically mispronounced a word in the script. A man leaned over to tell him the correct pronunciation. His name was Quincy Jones. Already a distinguished talent by the time he met Michael, Jones was a musician, producer and songwriter who began his career in the 1950s touring as a jazz musician with acts such as Dizzy Gillespie. He had won his first Grammy in 1963 for his arrangement of the song 'I Can't Stop Loving You' and, along with Bob Russell, became the first African-American to be nominated for an Academy Award in the Best Original Song category. Having corrected Michael on the word in the script of *The Wiz*, he left the singer with an open offer for help in the future. Just over a year later, Michael picked up the phone, dialled Jones's number and took him up on it. Jones had made a rather fortunate habit of meeting future stars when they were twelve years of age. He had first encountered Aretha Franklin and Stevie Wonder at that age. Now he had met Michael, too. 'I was fully aware of Michael and impressed by the achievements that he'd reached with the Jackson 5, but it never crossed my mind that we would eventually work together,' he recalled later in the *Los Angeles Times*. 'But as is always the case, divinity interceded into the process.'

Given the creative and financial riches that lay ahead for the partnership, it is interesting that both Michael and Jones lacked confidence in his potential when they started working together. True, Michael had released solo material before, but that was very much under the umbrella of The Jackson 5/The Jacksons. Here, he felt, he was truly branching out on his own and he felt a sense of vulnerability as he did so. Jones was not convinced that Michael would be an enormous solo success, though he was mightily impressed by the artist's work ethic and focus. For instance, Michael preferred to learn lyrics by heart rather than read them off a sheet of paper during recording. Furthermore, when recording the sad track 'She's Out of My Life', he cried into the microphone at the conclusion of each take. Soon, their relationship went beyond that of artist/producer to become an almost father-and-son rapport. That Michael was allowed substantial creative input into the recording sessions, which took place at Allen Zentz Recording, Westlake Audio and Cherokee Studios in Los Angeles, made him very happy. At these venues Jones encountered a similar shyness and vulnerability in Michael to that witnessed by Sidney Lumet and his guests. 'He was so shy he'd sit down and sing behind the couch with his back to me while I sat there with my hands over my eyes with the lights off,' remembered Jones in *Michael Jackson: The Magic and the Madness*.

A song that only existed thanks to Michael's creative input was the classic 'Don't Stop 'Til You Get Enough'. He had, he said, been struck by the infectious melody while in his kitchen one day. When he played Jones a recording of the tune, they agreed to put the song on the album. Once Michael had written the lyrics, the pair were sure they had a major hit on their hands. Less impressed was Michael's mother Katherine, who found the song's lyrics sexually suggestive. He assured his mother that the song was not about sex, and could refer to any activity the listener wanted. The song was indeed a hit, reaching number one in America and several other countries. It was also his breakthrough release in Germany, where it reached number thirteen. Other stand-out tracks from the sessions included 'Rock with You' – which became the bestselling single of 1980 in America – and 'Off the Wall', both written by Rod Temperton; the Paul McCartney-penned 'Girlfriend'; 'She's Out of My Life' by Tom Bahler; and 'I Can't Help It' by Motown legend Stevie Wonder.

All of these tracks appeared on the resultant album *Off the Wall*, which was released on 10 August 1979, just weeks before Michael's twenty-first birthday. (He celebrated that milestone with a bash at Studio 54 in New York City, and a slew of magazines covered his celebration.) The album was immediately hailed as a classic by the critics. Stephen Holden of *Rolling Stone* magazine wrote that the album was: 'A triumph for producer Quincy Jones as well as for Michael Jackson, *Off the Wall* represents discofied post-Motown glamour at its classiest.' Meanwhile, Phil McNeil of *Melody Maker* also praised the record, concluding that Michael was 'probably the best singer in the world right now in terms of style and technique'. It was an enormously significant album not just for Michael but also for the music industry. Here, black disco music was brought to a more mainstream audience than ever before. And for Michael it was hugely important, revitalizing his career: it is worth noting that previously Michael's sales figures, both solo and with the band, had been slipping. Jones admits that he had by no means banked on the album performing so well. 'Anyone who tells you that they knew a record was going to be a big hit is a flat-out liar,' he insisted in the *Los Angeles Times*. 'We had no idea *Off the Wall* was going to be as successful as it was, but we were thrilled.' However, even in the face of substantial critical praise and commercial success, Michael was unsatisfied. When *Rolling Stone* told his publicist that they did not feel he was cover-star material, Michael was furious. 'Just wait,' he snapped, 'some day those magazines are going to be begging me for an interview.'

The album made the top five in America and Britain and ultimately sold more than 20 million copies around the world. However, it was with the singles from the album that Michael truly did well. 'Don't Stop 'Til You Get Enough', 'Rock with You', 'Off the Wall' and 'She's Out of My Life' all went to number one in America, making him the first solo act to have four number-one singles from one album. Michael became a millionaire off the back of the success. He later also won a Grammy, the first of his career – although he would feel bitter disappointment that he only netted one for the album. 'This can never happen again,' he said of his failure to triumph in the Album of the Year category, and he boycotted the ceremony in protest at what he felt was a pigeonholing of his work. All the same, his confidence was soaring and he soon appointed his own lawyer – New York man John Branca, who had been instructed by Bob Dylan and The Beach Boys. One of his first tasks was to renegotiate the royalty terms with CBS, and he secured his client the highest rate in the music industry: 37 per cent – a far cry from the Motown contract which afforded him just one-fifth of the Jackson brothers' 6 per cent. Signing up with Branca was yet another step away from the grip of his father for Michael. Their relationship had been strained further by Joseph's continued infidelities, one of which had spawned a daughter called Joh'Vonnie to the dismay of Katherine and the Jackson brothers. The singer found this particularly upsetting, and was about to embark on a course of action that some interpreted as his way of distancing himself from his father.

* * *

In 1979, Michael slipped while dancing onstage and broke his nose. He flew to Los Angeles where he had his first nose-job operation. For years he had been uncomfortable about the size of his nose, and had been teased by his father and his brothers. Now he had a chance to do something about it. 'The greatest joy I ever had was in knowing I had a choice about my face,' he was to say later. He was happy with the visual results of the surgery but the operation was not entirely successful. In its wake he was finding it harder to breathe and that problem came worryingly to the fore when he was singing. So he went for a second operation on his nose, which changed his appearance even more. He had not informed his family of this treatment – administered by Santa

Monica surgeon Dr Steven Hoefflin, who would perform many future operations on Michael – and when he returned home bandaged and bruised, his mother at first thought he had been injured. He retired to his bedroom for a week, to be occasionally glimpsed in the kitchen over the coming days, gathering a snack of vegetarian food. (Tired of his acne, he had followed the example of Jermaine, whose vegetarianism had cleared up his skin blotches.)

Why was Michael so uncomfortable with his appearance? Some friends speculated that he was aiming to appear like his hero, friend and mentor Diana Ross. Others assumed that he was simply responding to the twin pressures of the scrutinizing eye of fame and the mockery to which his brothers and – in particular – his father had subjected him regarding his appearance. A third theory, and one that perhaps holds more weight, was that he was in fact acting in response to an anxiety that he might turn out to look like his father. Many young men are determined to not turn into their fathers but for Michael, still terrified of his father's physical and emotional bullying, and horrified by his infidelity, this feeling was especially powerful. However, these two early operations on his nose were but the tip of the iceberg as his appearance was to change regularly and dramatically in the decades that remained of his life. Thanks to this fact, and his bizarre denials that he had had any purely cosmetic surgery, his face became a major talking point.

The media was becoming ever more intrigued by Michael. His nose operations were clear to anyone paying attention – the album cover for *Off the Wall* showed Michael's nose had changed since his Jackson 5 days. The pitch of his voice prompted chatter too.

Speculation mounted that he was taking female hormones in order to keep his voice high. 'Not true,' his voice coach Seth Riggs told *Time* magazine. 'I'm his voice teacher, and I'd know. He started out with a high voice, and I've taken it even higher. He can sing low – down to a basso low C – but he prefers to sing as high as he does because pop tenors have more range to create style.' A rumour also started to the effect that Michael had undergone a sex change, and his sister Janet was later to claim that a female fan had committed suicide on hearing the rumour.

Just as his appearance and voice became the subject of feverish conjecture, so too did his increasingly unconventional personality fascinate the media. Already, at the age of twenty-two, he was showing signs of the eccentric, childlike qualities that would become so big a part of his public image. While most men that age begin to leave behind the ways of childhood, Michael seemed to embrace them ever tighter. The signs began to show themselves gradually but increasingly strongly. He pasted his bedroom walls with pictures of Peter Pan and cried when telling people how much he related to 'the lost boy of Never-Never Land'. He later told an interviewer he *was* Peter Pan. Likewise, when he 'met' the eponymous alien star of Steven Spielberg's film *E.T.*, Michael seemed to believe that the model was real. The director noticed him talking to the puppet and the singer complained in the days after that he was missing his new friend. He said the film reminded him of himself. 'The whole story,' he told *Smash Hits* magazine. 'You know, someone from another world coming down and you becoming friends with them and this person's like eight hundred years old and he's filling you with all kinds of wisdom and he's magic and he can teach you how to fly.' He spoke in similar terms of rats, around the time of the release of 'Ben'. 'I love rats, you know,' he told reporters, 'I really do feel like I'm talking to a friend when I play with them.' In November 1982 he shared the cover of *Ebony* magazine with the *ET* model.

* * *

From the start of his fame, Michael's age had been an issue. When the Jackson brothers signed with Motown, two years were shaved off his age. True, his brothers' ages were adjusted as well but with Michael as the front man and baby-face of the band, the spin on his age had always been most pronounced. The label had been very stringent in casting him as the young and cute one. As a young man moves from his teenage years into his early twenties, any childish ways he retained would normally be discouraged by those closest to him. However, with Michael they were at best overlooked and at worst encouraged by his nearest. 'If any artist loses that childlikeness, you lose a lot of creative juice,' said Jane Fonda in the *Guardian* after a week with the star. Soon he was seen playing with toys and children's board games. He also began to invite inside child fans who waited outside his home to talk to him. He spoke admiringly of children and their 'genius'. But with sadness, he added: 'When they become a certain age, they lose it.' No wonder that the media were soon dubbing him a 'man-boy' and a 'man-child'. The sight of this already iconic celebrity responding to his fame not by bedding women, but by sitting and talking to children was peculiar.

The pressure of the public eye began to tell on Michael in his dealings with the press. J Randy Taraborrelli was sent to interview Michael in the autumn of 1981. Taraborrelli was already well-known to Michael and his family, having interviewed them on a number of occasions. In his biography of Michael, first published in 1991, the journalist recalls that for this interview Michael had a bizarre demand: Taraborrelli would ask his questions to Janet, who would repeat them to Michael, and Janet would then repeat the subsequent answer to Taraborrelli. At no point could the journalist quiz Michael directly. It was a peculiar way for any interview to be conducted, not least one with a familiar and trusted journalist. Taraborrelli was therefore forced to ask: 'Janet, would you please ask him how he feels about the album?' She then asked her brother: 'He wants to know how you feel about the album.' After she repeated Michael's subsequent response to the journalist, her brother pointed out that she had forgotten to include one word of the answer. However, he refused to drop the frustrating terms of the interview and eventually Taraborrelli gave up and went home. The 'interview' never appeared in print. He later put another odd stipulation on a television interview: he would only conduct it in total darkness. All the same, his draw for the media was growing: the same year as the Taraborrelli 'interview', Michael made the cover of the UK music magazine *New Musical Express* (*NME*) and was interviewed for the title by a young Danny Baker.

Soon, it would be time for Michael and Quincy Jones to head into the Westlake Studios and commence work on his second album together. *Off the Wall* had been a commercial and critical success, but nobody could be prepared for what their next project would produce, creatively and commercially. The duo had over three hundred songs to choose from for the forthcoming album: the nine they selected were to make musical history and set records that will probably never be broken. It is interesting that in *The Wiz*, the movie that brought artist and producer together, Michael's character says: 'Success, fame, and fortune, they're all illusions.' Illusions or not, he was about to experience phenomenal amounts of all three of those things thanks to the response to his next album. When he first met with his lawyer, Branca, Michael had told him that he wanted to be the 'biggest and the wealthiest' star in the world of entertainment. This was the album that would help him achieve his goal.

However, *Thriller* did not have an entirely smooth path from conception to release. Jones and the other members of the team working with Michael on the album were keen to manage his expectations. One day they asked him how he would feel if the new record did not perform as well as *Off the Wall*, another time they warned him that he should not expect more than 2 million in sales. Michael was hurt and enraged, telling them that he expected it to be the highest-selling album of all time, a dream he had held since childhood. They laughed at his optimism and he was soon threatening to cancel the entire project, so furious was he at their words of caution. In the end, the top brass of CBS were called in to massage Michael's wounded ego so he would continue recording. True, he was proving something of a diva, but his ambition and attention to detail were also clear for all to see. Michael was focused, professional and driven: he refused to take a lazy approach to the making of an album. 'People used to do an album where you'd get one good song, and the rest were like B-sides,' he told the *Mirror*. 'They'd call them "album songs" – and I would say to myself, "Why can't every one be like a hit song? Why can't every song be so great that people would want to buy it as a single?" So I always tried to strive for that. That was my purpose for the next album. I'm a perfectionist. I'll work until I drop. And I worked so hard on that album.' Of that there can be no doubt, he did indeed work hard, and some remarkable songs were emerging from the recording sessions.

Among these was a song that Michael had written during the sessions for *Off the Wall*, but held back. It was called 'Wanna Be Startin' Somethin'', and in the lyrics Michael vented his fury at the gossip grapevine of which he was so often the victim. It was a classic concert-opening number, and became the familiar debut song on several world tours he undertook. It also built into an infectious, memorable African chant: 'Mama-se, mama-sa, ma-ma-coo-sa', which became iconic for generations, and was sampled by twenty-first-century pop star Rihanna, who was not even born when *Thriller* was released. A song with a theme that also dealt with the pitfalls of fame was 'Billie Jean', which Michael wrote after a real-life mentally ill female fan dishonestly claimed he had fathered her child and further suggested that mother, son and 'father' should enter a suicide pact together. However, producer Jones was not impressed enough by the song to believe it merited a place on the album. Even once Michael insisted, his producer suggested they change the name so it was not mistakenly believed to be about the tennis icon of the 1960s and 1970s, Billie Jean King. Michael had been so mesmerized by the melody of the song when he was writing it that he managed to drive down a motorway oblivious to the fact that his Rolls-Royce's engine was in flames. A motorcyclist pointed out the problem before tragedy could strike. The song was reportedly mixed ninety-one times by Bruce Swedien, before he eventually chose the second mix.

Another of the album tracks penned by Michael was 'Beat It', which brought a new rocky edge to the Jackson sound. Jones had been encouraging the inclusion of such a number and even though Michael knew he had written a song that fitted his producer's brief, he was at first too shy to reveal the song he had written. Legendary guitarist Eddie Van Halen – who had initially assumed that Jones's telephoned approach to him was a practical joke – provided the guitar line for free. 'I did it as a favour,' he says in *Michael Jackson: For the Record*. He disputes that his non-paying performance meant Michael had taken advantage of him. 'I was a complete fool, according to the rest of the band, our manager and everyone else. I knew what I was doing – I don't do something unless I want to do it.' The accompanying video was shot in the rough environs of Skid Row in Los Angeles and used genuine gang members. An all-round tamer affair – 'The Girl Is Mine' – was co-written by Michael and Paul McCartney. The pair put it together while watching cartoons, and the song did indeed have a distinctly gentle feel, which was observed by critics and by many of Michael's black fans, who suspected he was pandering to white tastes. However, Michael remained unapologetic, not least because he had so enjoyed recording with McCartney. 'One of my favourite songs to record, of all my recordings as a solo artist, is probably "The Girl Is Mine,"' he says in *Michael Jackson: For the Record*.

'Working with Paul McCartney was pretty exciting and we just literally had fun…it was like lots of kibitzing and playing and throwing stuff at each other and making jokes.'

The album's title track, 'Thriller', was written by Rod Temperton. It was originally called 'Starlight', but the title and with it the feel of the song was changed during the recording to become the sinister, horror-movie-themed track that became so popular across the globe. Vincent Price, the actor so synonymous with that genre, was hired to provide a chilling spoken 'outro', which culminated in his evil cackles. In common with Jones and other members of the production team, Price had no idea at this stage how huge Michael's album would become. 'I didn't think anything would happen with it,' he remembered. How wrong he was – it was about to become one of the decade's most iconic pop tunes and one of pop's most celebrated songs ever. Michael had known Price since he was just eleven years old, and told *Smash Hits* he was the only choice for the outro. 'I mean, who's the king of horror who's still alive?' he said. 'I mean [Dracula actor] Bela Lugosi and [player of numerous sinister movie roles] Peter Lorre are dead now and the only giant who goes back to those days is Vincent Price – so I thought he was the perfect voice.'

With CBS anxious to release the album as soon as possible, Michael and his crew came under enormous pressure to finish the project. However, when he was played the 'finished' product, Michael was not happy. As they sat in Westlake Studios, tears flowed down his face. Against shouted protests from CBS employees, he ordered that it be remixed and only once this had been done to his satisfaction did Michael agree to hand it over to the label. *Thriller* was released on 30 November 1982 and quickly fulfilled Michael's predictions in terms of sales. Having been warned to expect no more than 2 million sales in total, Michael was delighted to learn that *Thriller* was soon selling as many as that in a single fortnight. 'I knew it,' smiled Michael, 'I just *knew* it.' It broke record after record: the first solo album to exceed 12 million sales; it won an unprecedented seven Grammys in 1984; it was the first album to include seven top ten singles. (Writing about this in *Smash Hits* magazine, Peter Martin quipped: 'I've just about had enough of this so-called Peter Bloody Pan Of Pop – 'P.Y.T.' is about the 643rd release from *Thriller*.') However, the greatest honour of all – and the one Michael had dreamed of for so long – came on 7 February 1984, when it was confirmed as the best-selling album of all time. 'Bust open the champagne,' cried Jones to Michael when the news reached them. It retains that record to this day.

Ironically, the press reception that greeted its release had not been entirely glowing by any means. Christopher Connelly of *Rolling Stone* magazine complained that 'the title song…degenerates into silly camp,' and concluded that the album was no more than 'a gorgeous, snappy step in the right direction'. *Melody Maker*'s Paolo Hewitt went even further, writing: 'Jackson seems to have lost his talent for turning gross into gold' – an incredible critical thumbs-down for an album that was to break commercial records. At least John Rockwell in the *New York Times* was more positive. '*Thriller* is a wonderful pop record, the latest statement by one of the great singers in popular music today,' he wrote, 'but it is more than that. It is as hopeful a sign as we have had yet that the destructive barriers that spring up regularly between white and black music – and between whites and blacks – in this culture may be breached once again.' Michael truly was becoming a trailblazer in a new era of hope for further harmony in the music industry.

Thriller was not only significant culturally. Michael's album proved to have a substantial legacy on the industry commercially, which was revived by the success of the album. 'The fallout from *Thriller* has given the [music] business its best years since the heady days of 1978, when it had an estimated total domestic revenue of $4.1 billion,' said a report in *Time* magazine. So *Thriller* was an epochal album all round: it opened up further racial harmony, revived the industry's flagging financial fortunes, and its lead single also revolutionized the music video arm of the business. To produce the video, Michael aimed high. Having watched and loved the 1981 John Landis-directed horror film *An American Werewolf in London*, he duly hired Landis to direct the video for 'Thriller', for which he envisaged a not dissimilar theme of ghoulish physical transformation in its star role. To meet the required budget for what was planned, Michael and his lawyer John Branca came up with the idea of releasing a 'making of' film of the 'Thriller' video to raise extra funds. This was an innovative move and the tape attracted advance orders of over 100,000. It sold over half a million copies in its first month on sale.

The video itself was a spectacular, fourteen-minute long affair that began with Michael warning his co-star (played by *Playboy* model Ola Ray) 'I'm not like other guys' and adding: 'I mean – I'm different.' Although he said this in character, there were fewer more true words spoken by the singer. They are joined by a troupe of dancing corpses who emerge from a cemetery. During the course of the video Michael transforms from a human into a zombie and then a werewolf. At the conclusion, all seems well when Michael returns to his normal human form and asks Ray what the problem was. As a final twist, he turns his back to her and grins at the camera demonically with scary yellow eyes. The video was to go down a storm in the industry, but before it was released Michael had been forced to weather a very personal storm that it had created.

Members of Michael's Jehovah's Witnesses church invited him to a meeting and, complaining that the video had satanic themes, insisted he distance himself from it. When he refused, they said they would exclude him from the church. He initially ordered his team to cancel the video and destroy all the tapes, which would have been an enormously costly turn of events. Instead, a compromise was reached when a disclaimer from Michael was added to the beginning of the video. It read: 'Due to my strong personal convictions, I wish to stress that this film in no way endorses a belief in the occult.' A more humorous disclaimer came at the end, at the suggestion of Landis: 'Any similarity to actual events or persons living, dead (or undead) is purely coincidental.' It had been a hair-raising experience for the character played by Michael's co-star Ray, and a surprising one for the model-turned-actress herself. 'I didn't know that I was going to be a part of history,' she said, 'but that is the way it turned out. I'm thankful.' As for Michael, he described it as the most fun video he ever made. 'I just loved becoming a monster, because it gave me a chance to pretty much become someone else,' he smiled. Indeed, one can see in the video how much fun he was having. One look into his eyes as he sings the opening line of the song shows them full of excitement.

MTV, the American music cable channel, had launched in 1981 and soon became defined by the 'Thriller' video, which it broadcast repeatedly. The video debuted in Britain on the Channel 4 show *The Tube*. Viewers in their millions stayed up until 1 a.m. on 3 December 1983 to watch it. The sales of the album were reignited by the popularity of the video, with Michael estimating that 14 million sales were created by the popularity of the video alone. The album was to spend eighty consecutive weeks in the American top ten. The video had reshaped how pop songs would be promoted. It also made Michael ever more famous and popular but it was not the only small-screen venture he used to catapult him to greater global fame. On 25 March 1983 the Pasadena Civic Center was the setting for a television special entitled *Motown 25: Yesterday, Today and Forever*, which featured a host of acts who had been part of the label's success, including Marvin Gaye, Stevie Wonder and The Supremes. It promised to be a star-studded night. The Jackson 5 reunited for the evening, too – complete with Jermaine. They sang several songs including 'I Want You Back' and – emotionally, given Jermaine's presence – 'I'll Be There'. The brothers embraced and all left the stage, apart from Michael. Little could the audience at the venue, nor the 47 million who watched on television around the world when it was broadcast a month later, know that they were about to witness an iconic performance by him, one that was arguably the finest moment of his career not just to date but ever.

The irony is that Michael had almost not appeared on the show and took a lot of convincing before agreeing to sign up. It was only when the producers told him that he could perform 'Billie Jean' – a non-Motown song – that he agreed. Once his brothers had left the stage, Michael launched into the song. He looked phenomenal, in a black sequined jacket that he had purchased during the recording of *Thriller*, and tight black trousers that revealed his white socks and gleaming black leather shoes. He also wore a single white glove on his left hand and dramatically added a black fedora to the ensemble as the song kicked in – to the delight of the audience, who also howled their approval when he theatrically dispensed with it. He later claimed he had choreographed his routine the previous evening in his kitchen at home. One would not have known it from his imperious, perfect delivery of it onstage – he had the audience in raptures throughout. The climax came towards the end when he performed in public for the first time his take on the 'Moonwalk' dance, in which he appeared to be moving forward while gliding backwards. It was enough to send the audience into further hysteria, even though he only Moonwalked briefly. As they responded to that dance, he spun round and leapt up, only to land on his toes in a dramatic hunched pose. It had been an extraordinary perform-ance, but as the audience raised the roof at its conclusion the perfectionist in Michael was unsatisfied, feeling he had not performed the spin part to the ideal standards he craved.

Backstage he was showered with excited praise. But there was a symbolic moment when Jackie shouted, 'The Jackson 5 are back,' just as Michael walked away from them. The plaudits continued to come his way for days on end, with even the legendary Fred Astaire calling Michael to add his praise. 'You're a hell of a mover,' he told Michael. 'Man, you really put them on their asses last night.' (Michael would later contribute to a book written about Astaire, and also dedicated his own autobiography to him.) Just as one icon was heaping compliments on him, so Michael was being grouped with other music legends. The newspapers were comparing him to Frank Sinatra and Elvis Presley. When the show was broadcast the following month, his performance was also being compared with other legendary televisual music moments, including the appearances on *The Ed Sullivan Show* by The Beatles and Elvis Presley. Much of Michael's performance was not new – he had first worn a single glove onstage in the 1970s and the Moonwalk dance had been around for decades – but the way he had pulled together and pulled off the outfit and dance moves was sensational, winning him many millions of new fans around the world in just four minutes. The Moonwalk became so associated with him that years later he would be asked to perform it to verify his identity when making a large purchase in a shop on credit card, while wearing a disguise. Likewise, by 1984 the 'single glove' part of his look had become synonymous with Michael, with New Jersey students protesting when they were banned from wearing single white gloves to school.

His next experience in front of the television cameras was far less enjoyable although it too would make his level of recognition soar. He had initially been uncomfortable about the soft drink manufacturer Pepsi's offer of a lucrative endorsement deal. According to Taraborrelli's book, he had snapped, 'I don't drink

Pepsi. I don't *believe* in Pepsi.' However, he eventually relented and agreed to take part in commercials for the drink alongside his brothers. Michael would personally earn £7 million for his involvement in the commercials which were shot at the Shrine Auditorium on West Jefferson Boulevard in Los Angeles. Three thousand fans were in attendance at the filming on 27 January 1984. On a day that was to prove disastrous for Michael, he created another personal drama backstage first. While using the toilet, he accidentally dropped his white glove into the bowl. The scream he emitted in horror at this could be heard for some distance. With the glove recovered and dried, filming could begin and with it an incident that put his dropping of the glove into perspective. Towards the end of the day, Michael was being filmed striding down some stairs while fireworks were set off behind him. The explosions were perilously close to his head, just two feet away, and his hair was set alight by the sparks. At first he did not realize he was on fire, believing that the intense heat he was feeling was due to the powerful spotlights trained on him. Some members of the audience, noting how calm he was, assumed that the flames were part of the act.

However, as he realized what was happening, Michael tried to smother the flames with his jacket. He then collapsed to the ground, leading his brother Jermaine to fear that he had been shot. Many members of the audience had come to the same conclusion and panic was spreading fast. The first person to reach Michael was Marlon Brando's son, Miko, who worked in the singer's security team. Brando doused the flames coming from Michael's hair, burning his own hands in the process. Meanwhile, quick-thinking Gary Stiffelman (one of Michael's management team) snatched the video tapes from the crew, so his side would have possession of all the footage of the incident. It was bedlam on the stage, with panicked cries and demands for ice. Michael was doused with a rug and then had ice applied to the affected area. Even in the midst of this pain, as he suffered second and third degree burns to his head, Michael was mindful of the enormous publicity opportunity he had on his hands. When an ambulance arrived he declined the chance to be loaded into it via a quiet, rear exit and insisted he leave the venue in view of the fans and media. As the ambulance team attempted to remove his white glove, he told them to leave it on because 'the media is here'. The footage of him leaving the venue on a stretcher was played around the world on news channels. He waved to the cameras and fans as the ambulance doors were about to be shut. One fan who was there said: 'He was wonderful. He reassured people even as he was being taken away on a stretcher.' Michael was in shock and pain, yet he had turned this incident into a public relations triumph.

He was taken to the Cedars-Sinai Medical Center on Beverly Boulevard and then moved to the Brotman Medical Center. In a twist of fate, only a few weeks earlier Michael had paid a visit to the burns unit of the Brotman. The establishment was given a crash course in the world of Michael. Thousands of cards, letters and gifts quickly arrived at the hospital, one of which came from President Ronald Reagan. According to some reports, another came from a fan called Jordan Chandler, then just four years of age. Chandler reportedly enclosed a photograph of himself with his well-wishing note, and was delighted when a few days later he received a reply from Michael telling him he was a 'beautiful young boy'. It was not the last contact the pair would have. Brotman was quickly forced to hire a new team of switchboard operators to deal with the bombardment of calls from concerned fans. Michael was quickly in good spirits, sitting up in bed and watching the science-fiction film *Close Encounters of the Third Kind*, chatting on the phone to friends and even singing as he showered. While at the Brotman he noticed a clear plastic chamber. He asked a doctor what it was. 'An oxygen chamber,' he was told. He learned more about how the chamber worked and stored the information away for future use. Plastic surgeon Steven Hoeffin – who had performed the singer's second nose operation – examined Michael and told reporters that he might require surgery to his head. 'He is in discomfort', he told the press after visiting his client. 'It will take a few weeks to determine the hair loss.'

In his autobiography *Moonwalk*, Michael boasted that rather than seeking revenge on Pepsi for the incident he was 'real nice about it'. However, in *Michael Jackson: The Magic and the Madness*, J. Randy Taraborrelli paints a different picture of the aftermath. Michael, he writes, angrily demanded that his people release the video tapes of the incident to the world's media. 'I'm gonna ruin Pepsi,' he snapped. 'After my fans see this tape, Pepsi will be history.' His advisers and family warned him against this course of action, but Michael was adamant. When the president of Pepsi asked Joseph to intervene and convince his son against the release, Joseph said wearily: 'Try telling Michael what to do these days, he does what he wants to.' Eventually he was dissuaded from releasing the footage but threatened Pepsi with a writ, prompting them to hand over $1.5 million, which he donated to the Brotman Burns Center.

Despite their fears that their brand would be ruined by the accident, Pepsi actually witnessed an upwards surge in sales in its wake. They returned to Michael and offered him the biggest endorsement fee to date – $12 million for four advertisements – getting him another entry in the *Guinness Book of World Records*. He was also added to the same tome in February 1984 when he became the biggest-selling solo artist of all time. To celebrate this feat, CBS put on a party for Michael at New York's Museum of Natural History, which overlooks Central Park. Over two thousand guests attended including Andy Warhol, Dustin Hoffman, Diana Ross, Bruce Springsteen and Jackie Onassis. Their invitations had been in the shape of a glove, to reflect Michael's iconic style of hand-wear. The Borough President of Manhattan, Andrew Stein, made 7 February – the day of the bash – 'Michael Jackson Day'. A telegram from American President and former Hollywood actor Ronald Reagan was read out. 'I was pleased to learn that you were not seriously hurt in your recent accident,' it began. 'I know from experience that these things can happen on the set – no matter how much caution is exercised. All over America, millions of people look up to you as an example. Your deep faith in God and adherence to traditional values are an inspiration to all of us,' it continued. 'You've gained quite a number of fans along the road since "I Want You Back", and [Reagan's wife] Nancy and I are among them. Keep up the good work, Michael. We're very happy for you.' Michael spoke briefly to the partygoers, saying that for the first time in his career, he felt 'accomplished'. Then Norris

McWhirter presented Michael with a first edition of the 1984 *Guinness Book of World Records* paperback.

He was bouncing back from the Pepsi affair with increased popularity, shifting 700,000 copies of *Thriller* in the months that followed. However, the episode had other, less happy legacies. 'That Pepsi commercial debacle was a seminal event in Michael Jackson's life,' Stuart Backerman, who later became his publicist, told the *Vancouver Sun*. 'He was in pain, deep, incredible pain, and he was prescribed Demerol. Like a lot of people who get prescription drugs, it turned into a semi-habit.' Was it here, some have since wondered, that the seeds of Michael's untimely death were sown? The Pepsi affair also made Michael even more self-conscious about his appearance. He returned to Dr Hoefflin and underwent a third operation on his nose, implicitly asking for it to be made more like Diana Ross's. Although he again appeared bruised in the immediate wake of the operation, his new look was soon being admired by no less a celebrity figure than actress Joan Collins. 'You know, I must get the name of his plastic surgeon,' she said to a friend after they had spoken with Michael at a party. 'I simply *adore* his nose.' Another famous woman to take interest in his ever-changing appearance was First Lady Nancy Reagan, who met Michael on the day he was presented with an award at the White House. But, as is often the case with Michael, the genesis of this event is not as straightforward as it was presented to the public.

As has been widely documented, the episode had begun when a member of Reagan's government asked Michael for permission to use a segment of 'Beat It' on an anti-drink-driving television and radio campaign. He refused at first, believing such a move would be 'tacky'. However, he then came up with a plan. He let them know that were he to be invited to the White House to meet the President and his wife, and be handed an award by the President, then he would gladly forget about his objection and allow 'Beat It' to be used in the commercials. So it was that on 14 May 1984, he proudly presented himself at the White House, with his eight security guards in tow and crowds of Jackson fans lining the perimeter of the property. Michael was wearing a jacket modelled on the uniform worn by lift operators at the Helmsley Palace Hotel in New York City. He humbly whispered his gratitude as the President handed him his award, which was inscribed: 'To Michael Jackson with appreciation for the outstanding example you have set for the youth of America and the world.' Little did the watching nation know the truth of why he was being honoured thus.

It was later, behind the scenes, that Mrs Reagan expressed her curiosity about Michael's face, speculating repeatedly to one of his entourage about what the extent was of the 'work' he'd had done and then commenting on Michael's image in general. At first the entourage member kept quiet, but eventually he sighed and confided to the First Lady: 'You don't know the half of it.' Among the general public there was no less fascination, but it was the question of Michael's sexuality that continued to cause the most puzzlement and speculation. Why was this twenty-six-year-old man, who had millions of devoted female fans across the globe, still single and thought to be a virgin? The man himself theorized that, having learned so much about sexuality as a child thanks to his father's errant behaviour and the strip joints The Jackson 5 performed in, he was 'free to concentrate on other aspects of my life as an adult' rather than sexuality. (According to his sister Janet Michael lost his virginity at the age of thirty-four.)

Statements such as this did nothing to dampen the public's growing level of curiosity. On the day of the White House ceremony, Michael had arrived with a young, good-looking man alongside him and when asked by one of his press advisers who his guest was he snapped that it was none of anyone's business. That associate was in his early twenties, but Michael had in recent years struck up friendships with males much younger, including the actor Emmanuel Lewis, who was just twelve when he was befriended by the singer. Lewis's parents became increasingly concerned about Michael's close relationship with their son, not least when the pair checked into a hotel together. He also made friends with a ten-year-old boy called Jonathan Spence, and was spotted cuddling him. He invited a schoolboy haemophilia sufferer and other sick boys to stay with him. Concern was already high about the nature of Michael's friendships with these boys. With hindsight, that concern was very well-grounded. It is a shame that more effort was not put in at this stage to find out precisely what was going on.

* * *

Yet back in the mid-1980s, the rumours were not that Michael was attracted to boys, but to other men. He had visited a gay bar in West Hollywood with a friend, and few believed that his relationships with women such as Tatum O'Neal were genuinely romantic. Diana Ross had caught him backstage one evening applying her make-up, though many read this as more to do with his worship of her than anything more wide-ranging. The comedian Eddie Murphy once performed a sketch on primetime television questioning whether Michael was secretly gay and a newspaper claimed he was dating gay pop star Boy George. Michael was furious and arranged a press conference to deny the growing rumours. He had long felt indignant at the speculation the media whipped up about him and wrote in *Moonwalk*: 'Much of what they print is a fabrication. It's enough to make you want to ask: "What happened to the truth? Did it go out of style?"' In the same book, he echoed the vow made at the press conference: 'One day I know I'll find the right woman and get married myself. I often look forward to having children.' An unremarkable ambition to have in the scheme of things, you might think – until you read on. 'In my fantasy,' he continued, 'I imagine myself with thirteen children.'

It is interesting that Michael had visited gay bars, because two of his best friends at this time were popular icons among the global gay community. He had befriended Liza Minnelli after moving to Hollywood back in the Jackson 5 days. It was an exciting, glittering association for him – not least because he had for so long been fascinated by Minnelli's mother, the tragic star Judy Garland. Michael and Minnelli were inseparable at numerous star-studded parties, even jokingly pretending to be 'an item' at times. Michael later introduced Minnelli to David Gest, the man who became her fourth husband, and was best man at their wedding in 2002.

Maid of honour at that ceremony was actress Elizabeth Taylor, another good friend of Michael. The pair met during the 1980s and bonded over the way their early-starting careers in show business had robbed them of their childhoods. They quickly developed an intense friendship which remained for the rest of Michael's life. Taylor became an obsession of his, and a friend to call on in times of trouble. As for the actress, she was drawn to the glamour and drama of Michael's life from the moment they met. Well, there was plenty of the latter to come.

Regardless of – or perhaps in part *because* of – the questions about his personal life, Michael's fame was rising – fast. During February, March and April 1984 alone he appeared on the cover of scores of influential publications including *Time, USA Today, Rock & Folk, National Enquirer, The Globe, Jet* and *Blues & Soul*. The *News of the World* supplement also slapped him on its front page, naming him 'The World's Hottest Property'. With his growing celebrity status, Michael was moving further and further away from his brothers, not just professionally but personally. The 1984 Victory Tour was to bring relations between them to an all-time low. Michael had always been extremely reluctant to take part in the tour with his brothers. Eventually he agreed and hoped that his involvement would send a message to his brothers that he still loved and valued them. Unfortunately, relations became so strained during the eventful tour that he simply isolated himself from them even more. The first date was in Kansas City on 6 July 1984 and by the time the fifty-five-date tour was over the brothers were at loggerheads. An experience that it was hoped would heal turned out to merely hurt.

One day during the tour, Michael demanded that a publicist working on the tour be dismissed and said he would refuse to perform until the publicist was fired. Literally minutes before that evening's show, after attempts to placate Michael had failed, the publicist was indeed dismissed. Michael was soon also travelling in separate cars and separate planes to his brothers. When a producer offered to film the tour for a later commercial release, Michael refused to sign the deal, to the despair of his far less financially well-off brothers. 'My goal for the Victory tour was to give each performance everything I could,' he claimed in *Moonwalk*. 'I felt on top of the world. I felt determined...It was a nice feeling playing with my brothers again. We were all together again.' However, the reality was that he was coming across as a man who keenly wanted to be somewhere else. The private truth could hardly have been more different to the smiley, glossy front that was being put on matters publicly.

The atmosphere between him and his brothers grew ever more embittered, and it was not helped after pop broadcaster Jonathan King said that Michael was outshining his 'not particularly talented' brothers, reflecting the view of many fans and commentators. He also took to flouting numerous tour protocol agreements, and demanded a room on a separate floor to his brothers as relations spiralled ever downwards. When talk began about extending the tour to take in Europe, Michael adamantly and tersely refused. His mood had not been helped by the death threats against him which had been received by a Knoxville newspaper, prompting the FBI to get involved. Michael performed the Knoxville dates in defiance of the threats. On stage during the final date of the tour – in Los Angeles on 9 December – Michael delivered a devastating coup de theatre: without warning his brothers, he announced that 'This is our last and final show, it's been a long twenty years and we love you all.' There were positives to be drawn from the tour for Michael, who donated his $5 million tour fee to charity. His solo music was brought to yet more fans (there was never a tour to promote *Thriller* but he performed tracks from that album during the Victory dates). Also, he became more accustomed to the adulation of his fans during the tour. Although he still found their excitement overwhelming, and at times embarrassing, he concluded in *Moonwalk*: 'I can understand it because I'd feel the same way if, for instance, I could have met Walt Disney or Charlie Chaplin.' Still, the tour had in so many ways been at best a disappointment for all concerned.

By this time he had been honoured when a star on Hollywood Boulevard was awarded to him. It was number 1,793 and located outside Mann's Chinese Theater, a prime position. He thus became the first person to – in effect – have two stars awarded to him, having received one as a member of The Jacksons in the 1970s. He was forced to abandon his acceptance speech due to fear for the safety of his fans. Despite his continued attempts to understand and come to terms with the hysterical elements in his fan base, Michael often complained of the public's perception of him. 'I think I have a goody-goody image in the press and I hate that, but it's hard to fight because I don't normally talk about myself,' he wrote in *Moonwalk*. He added: 'I am a shy person. It's true. I don't like giving interviews or appearing on talk shows.' As well as bemoaning his public image, he also mourned the level of attention the media gave him. 'Consider that you really have no privacy,' he continued. 'The media prints whatever you say. They report whatever you do. I think my image gets distorted in the public's mind.' There was perhaps an element of dishonesty, or at best hypocrisy, to his complaints. Soon, he would become personally responsible for a slew of outlandish media stories about him which would further distort public perception of him and intensify the focus on him yet further.

The cult of Wacko Jacko was about to be born...

CHAPTER THREE

'The pressure of success does funny things to people,' wrote Michael in *Moonwalk*. It was meant as much as an observatory comment about others, rather than a purely self-searching assessment. Increasingly, though, that pressure appeared to be doing some very strange things to Michael himself. He had already transformed from 'Michael Jackson – child star' to 'Michael Jackson – pop star'. Soon, he would be dubbed, simply, 'Wacko Jacko', as he acquired a reputation as a distinctly oddball character. 'This is when the weirdness began to reach mythic proportions,' said Robert Thompson, an American professor of popular culture. Michael claimed to be frustrated and puzzled by this growing image and the stories that fuelled it. In truth, though, he was often a co-conspirator with the media and behind many of the wilder reports. 'Why not just tell people I'm an alien from Mars,' he snapped to biographer J. Randy Taraborrelli. 'Tell them I eat live chickens and do a voodoo dance at midnight.' Michael himself had indirectly told them things that were scarcely less potty.

He already had a kooky reputation in 1984, when UK magazine *Melody Maker* named him in its list of 'Ten Fruitcakes'. The following year, he obtained a new companion in his life – a chimpanzee called Bubbles. He adopted him at the age of three. There are conflicting stories as to how Michael obtained the chimpanzee. Some claim Michael rescued him from a cancer research clinic in Texas. Other stories suggest that after noticing the chimpanzee during its appearance in the American film *Back to School*, he purchased him from the filmmakers. Either way, he was excited to obtain the chimpanzee. Michael and his pet became inseparable, their bond exceeding even the sort of human/pet rapport he had sung about in 'Ben' in 1972. Bubbles and Michael ate together at the same dining table – '[the chimp] has great table manners,' reported Quincy Jones – and often wore the same clothes. The chimp slept in a cot at the end of his owner's bed and used his private bathroom, which was adorned with marble and gold. Michael told friends that he thought of the chimp as his 'first child' and claimed that Bubbles had tidied his bedroom for him. Michael himself also took to appearing in public wearing a gorilla mask over his head and, thus attired, he once humiliatingly fell over in view of an army of press photographers because his vision was obscured. He always enjoyed disguises, and once attended a Kool & the Gang concert at Radio City Music Hall in New York wearing an Afro wig and fake beard. Another occasion when a disguise led to discomfort came in 1989 when a heavily disguised Michael was grabbed by armed police who assumed from his odd appearance that he was a shoplifter.

Soon the 'monkey madness' was out of hand. Whereas most stars turned up to celebrity functions with a partner on their arm, Michael would arrive with Bubbles the chimp. The media began to write about Bubbles as they would a human superstar. He was rumoured to have his own bodyguard and an agent. Reports claimed he attended a local school every day, learning alongside the kids. Then the media speculated that Michael in fact owned several chimps called Bubbles, not just one. The controversial American artist Jeff Koons made a series of sculptures of Michael and Bubbles sitting together, one of which later attracted bids in excess of $5 million at auction. What a strange friendship. 'We all seek out individuals who are like us as friends,' explained animal expert Jennifer Viegas on the Discovery Channel, 'but I think Jackson had such an extraordinary life that he had trouble finding anyone to truly bond with. My guess is that he could project his need to care for another onto Bubbles, at least during this period.' The singer and his animal friend continued to be a source of endless fevered discussion across the world. True, his music had jetted him into our imaginations, but he was remaining there thanks to news coverage of stories such as those about Bubbles. The media frenzy that surrounded him was intense and prompted allegations of racism from Reverend Al Sharpton of the National Youth Movement. He said that Michael and his brothers were being punished by the media for 'not staying in the plantation of the music business'. The same month, the Kremlin accused Michael of being a stooge of the American government, employed to distract the public from unemployment and other issues.

As his global media superstardom soared, Michael's ambition was correspondingly all-encompassing. In 1986, he sensed a merchandizing opportunity in the public fascination over his animal companions. So he launched a series of stuffed toys entitled

'Michael's Pets', which included a frog called Uncle Tookie, a rabbit named Suzy, snakes, ostriches, giraffes and a llama called Louie – as well as a chimp called Bubbles. This was not his first merchandizing foray: in May 1984, Michael Jackson dolls had gone on sale in American stores for $12 each. In the same month he issued a civil suit against peddlers of unofficial merchandize in New York City. His lawyer Stephen Huff said: 'He is concerned that the public doesn't get cheap, inferior goods.' If the official doll range was to continue, it would have had to be regularly updated as the singer they were modelled on underwent yet more plastic surgery, with him presenting himself once more to Dr Hoefflin's clinic for a fourth nose job and to have a dent put into his chin. In the wake of that operation he also started to pluck his eyebrows and this – together with his decreasing weight due to a stringently followed diet – gave him a more defined facial appearance. His skin was beginning to lighten, too – the legacy of the bleaching cream he would apply to it, though he denied ever doing this.

There were plenty more Wacko Jacko stories on the horizon, but first he was to return to the recording studio to work on a very special project. He had been recruited by Lionel Richie to co-write a song which would raise funds for the starving people of Africa. It had been inspired by the British charity single 'Do They Know It's Christmas?', which was released in November 1984 and sold a million copies in its first week in the shops. Richie joined Michael at the family home and the duo spent a week composing the song, which would be called 'We Are the World'. According to LaToya, most of the lyrics were written by Michael. Soon after the song's completion, a 'super group' of American artists was put together to record it. The stellar line-up included Tina Turner, Billy Joel, Bruce Springsteen, Diana Ross and Bob Dylan. Also included were Michael's siblings Jackie, Marlon, Tito, Randy and LaToya. To complete the 'family affair' atmosphere for Michael, Jones was called in to produce the single.

On the evening of the recording, at the A&M Studios in Hollywood, there was a difficult moment when many of the ensemble's male vocalists found they could not reach the key that the chorus was set in. The key was altered and recording could continue. It had been the only tricky moment of a generally smooth-running evening, apart from the non-attendance of one performer: Prince. Michael would not have been disappointed by the absenteeism, as he was not fond of the singer. Sir Bob Geldof watched Michael rehearsing the song in a number of different keys and was deeply impressed. 'Each one was perfect,' he recalled in his book *Is That It?* There had been expectations that squeezing so many high-profile artists into one recording studio might lead to a clash of egos, but as it transpired the opposite happened and these world-famous acts were soon asking each other for autographs, so relaxed was the atmosphere. 'Everyone wanted a memento,' smiled Kenny Rogers. Stevie Wonder described the atmosphere as like 'something out of a dream'.

Perhaps the only display of ego on show – a sign reading 'Please check your egos at the door' had been placed outside the studio – came from Michael, who kept his sunglasses on throughout the evening. He had movingly addressed the assembled acts, telling them that he had written the song 'to inspire concern about a faraway place close to home'. In *Moonwalk* he speaks of artists on the night being 'united by our desire to make a difference'. However, the camera crew that recorded the event for a promotional video were asked to film Michael's lines on another occasion, when the other artists were not present. He personally directed the filming of his cameo, in which the camera began at his feet and swept upwards. He boasted privately that, unlike the other artists involved, he would be recognisable from his socks alone. Nothing can detract from the success of the single, though. It reached number one in America, the UK and other countries, eventually selling in excess of 7 million copies and winning four Grammys.

Next up for Michael came a foray into cinema. He describes the short film *Captain EO* as being about 'a young guy who goes on a mission...entrusted with the responsibility of bringing the inhabitants light and beauty'. It's not hard to see why he wanted to star in it. His involvement had come about when he met with Disney Studios to discuss the possibility of him designing a new ride to go in their theme parks. When discussion moved to the possibility of him appearing on-screen, movie-mad Michael jumped at the chance. Although only seventeen minutes long, *Captain EO* was an expensive affair, costing an estimated $30 million and taking one year to produce. As with the production of *The Wiz*, Michael is remembered by cast and crew as a dedicated worker. 'It was electrifying, the energy you felt off of him,' co-star Marlene Lang Clayman remembered in *Entertainment Weekly*. 'He gave one hundred per cent, every time.' The film was far from memorable, though Michael did not stop that from declaring in its wake that he saw his future in the movie industry, which he predicted he could bring a lot to. 'I'm going to try to make some changes,' he promised in *Moonwalk*. 'I'm going to try to change things round someday.' He was soon rumoured to be taking the lead role in numerous films including the Stephen Spielberg production of *The Phantom of the Opera*. It was during the making of *Captain EO* that he first met Karen Faye, his hair and make-up artist. He was subsequently reported to be dating her, but the pair were never more than friends.

In reality, the most significant legacy of the film was a stunt that Michael pulled to help publicize it. After seeing the oxygen chamber at Brotman Medical Center while being treated for his burns after the Pepsi accident, Michael had been told that sleeping in it could dramatically extend the length of one's life. Naturally this appealed to him, playing to his love of science fiction and affording the opportunity of moving closer towards a dream of eternal life (with a straight face, he later told TV interviewer Martin Bashir, 'I want to live forever'). He was dissuaded from purchasing a chamber, but had been photographed lying in it. Soon, a journalist at the US tabloid the *National Enquirer* was sniffing round the story but could not make it stand up enough to publish it. Just over two years later, though, an exciting related news item fell into his lap when Michael stage-managed its release to the media.

Via a new press manager especially hired for the occasion, Michael let it be known in the *National Enquirer* that he was sleeping in the chamber in a bid to live until he was at least 150 years old. He was, so the story went, planning to take the chamber on tour with him. Charles Montgomery, the *National Enquirer* journalist who received Michael's tip-off and wrote the piece, says he was specifically encouraged by Michael's press team to include the word 'wacky' in his report. A photograph of Michael in the chamber was provided, along with separate photos of the chamber empty. As the *National Enquirer* story spread like wildfire round the world's media, there were even some extra details added to spice it up, among them that Michael and his manager Frank DiLeo were supposedly at bitter loggerheads over the safety of the chamber. 'I told Michael that damn machine is too dangerous,' DiLeo told the Associated Press, playing his part in the spin. When *Rolling Stone* magazine called he continued in this vein, saying: 'I'm one hundred per cent against [the chamber]. I don't want it around.' He later told *Smash Hits* magazine that he was banning Michael from taking the chamber on the *Bad* tour.

Michael was jubilant. To the delight of his megalomaniac side, he believed that he could manipulate the world media. 'We can actually *control* the press,' he told his team. It was true he could in a sense do just that with the correct type of story, albeit at the cost of his image becoming ever stranger in the public eye. Nonetheless, he continued to spread similar stories of loopy behaviour to the media. Only later would he regret promoting these wacky fabrications, when he grew to hate the Wacko Jacko tag he'd been given and came to realize that any control he had over the media was only temporary. Once roused by the sniff of 'wackiness', the press proved a hard beast to tame. Like so many modern celebrities, he struggled with a contradictory relationship with the media, adoring the positive side of his fame, disliking the negative side and not accepting that they were two sides of the same coin.

When he came to promote his next album, more tales of Jackson wackiness would appear in the media, with his fingerprints all over them. First, though, he had to complete the making of the record. Whereas there was a three-year gap between *Off the Wall* and *Thriller*, the hiatus between *Thriller* and its successor was five years. 'Quincy [Jones] and I decided that this album should be as close to perfect as humanly possible,' wrote Michael in *Moonwalk*, explaining the longer production period awarded to it. 'A perfectionist has to take his time; he shapes and he [moulds] and he sculpts that thing until it's perfect. He can't let go before he's satisfied; he can't.' Work began in the summer of 1986, with the enormously successful, rich and famous Michael still only twenty-seven years old. He admits that during the making of the album, he and Jones fought over a number of issues. Given the phenomenal success of *Thriller*, Michael was under a lot of pressure to produce an album to surpass that record-breaking classic. He said this did not trouble him, as he felt he created his best work when under pressure. This might be the reason why he reportedly stuck a note reading '100 million' on his bathroom mirror during the recording of *Bad*.

Perhaps the pressure was telling on him, though. Michael tried to set up numerous duets with other stars for the album, the attraction of which would appear to be increasing the commercial appeal of the album via a backdoor. However, to his surprised disappointment, he was turned down by Barbra Streisand, Whitney Houston and Prince, with whom he wanted to vocally joust on the title track. That third rejection – which came after an extraordinarily tense summit between the two artists – particularly disappointed Michael as he had an entire press game in his mind to accompany the partnership. He would place stories in the press that he and Prince were fighting and then – lo and behold – a month later he would unveil the single on which they vocally collaborated. It was not to be. He had also been confident of convincing Streisand to duet with him. He had told *Smash Hits* it was a done deal: 'We're going to be doing a duet together,' he said. 'We'll be writing it together.'

In the end Michael sang alone on all eleven tracks, nine of which he wrote himself. The album's title track was naturally a stand-out, prompting discussion as to whether he was declaring himself 'bad' in the traditional sense of the word, or in the modern slang sense – i.e. good. 'Man in the Mirror' was another classic from the album, in which Michael urges listeners to change themselves before they try to change the world around them. In *Moonwalk*, his sense of personal grandeur is palpable when discussing this song. 'If John Lennon was alive, he could really relate to that song,' he wrote. 'It's the same thing [JF] Kennedy was talking about when he said, "Ask not what your country can do for you; ask what you can do for your country."' He added that he believed the song also tallied with the lives and messages of Martin Luther King and Mahatma Gandhi. These were grandiose comparisons to draw but the song was instantly popular, and its release as a single won a Grammy nomination in the Record of the Year category. (This was to be one of the last times that such a self-effacing theme would be heard in Michael's music. In the future this would be replaced by self-aggrandising and paranoid talk of conspiracies.)

The album was completed in July 1987 and was ready to be unveiled to an expectant public and press upon its August release date. 'What could Michael Jackson do to follow up the best-selling album to date?' asked the *New York Times* on the eve of its release.

It was a good question, and when the critics gave their verdict, this dimension was reflected. The *New York Times*, for instance, published a review that rather sat on the fence in its judgement. '*Bad* doesn't aim for as many emotional extremes as *Thriller*. It's a well-made, catchy dance record by an enigmatic pop star. And its commercial fate depends on whether Mr. Jackson's audience wants shadows along with smooth surfaces.' Of 'Man in the Mirror', the review continued: 'Snipers have dismissed this as a solipsistic, Eighties view of political engagement, but no one since Dylan has written an anthem of community action that has moved so many as Michael's (and Lionel's) "We Are the World". And no such grandiose plans can succeed without the first, private steps that Michael describes here.'

It was not just the critics who zoomed in on Michael at this time, the news reporters of the tabloid-style media did also. The influential *People* magazine ran a cover feature on Michael, with the strap-line asking: 'Is this guy weird, or what?' One story that had fuelled the flames of this increasing perception of Michael came about as a result of his love of a classic American movie. *The Elephant Man*, directed by David Lynch, is a true tale of a physically deformed man who lived in London in the nineteenth century. The lead character is the ultimate interloper, struggling to gain the understanding of a cruel public. Michael related to this. 'I saw a lot of similarities between our stories,' he said. He was in tears the first time he watched it, and his interest in the film prevailed for many years. He also watched the Broadway production of *The Elephant Man*, starring David Bowie. He began to investigate the life of Joseph Merrick – who was known as John Merrick in the film –

and visited London Hospital Medical College, where his skeleton was housed, in 1982 and 1985. (During the latter visit to England's capital he caused chaos, with over eight thousand fans arriving to try to catch a glimpse of him as he left Madame Tussaud's where a wax model of him had been built.) He bought rare books about Merrick's life, including one called *The Elephant Man and Other Stories* by Sir Frederick Treves, an acquaintance of Merrick. He also began to visit a hospital in America to personally watch operations – including brain surgery – being conducted on patients.

During the run-up to the release of *Bad*, Michael was considering ways of drumming up some publicity, just as he had prior to the release of *Captain EO*. Remembering his visits to Merrick's skeleton, he decided to release a story claiming he had tabled a bid of $500,000 for the bones of Joseph Merrick. Naturally the media leapt on this, as more proof of Michael's continued eccentricity. However, the same reporters quoted a representative of the college as saying no such bid had been received by them. To keep the news item alive, Michael then opted to make an offer for the skeleton, of double what the media had reported: $1 million. However, the bid was rejected out of hand, as the college's chief administrator David Edwards told CBC Radio. 'We don't encourage people to take a morbid interest in [the skeleton],' he said. 'I understand [Michael] wants to have the skeleton at home, alongside other exhibits and the question of him having him frankly doesn't arise with us.'

This was not a problem for Michael; he was content just to have created another media storm around his image, this time in the run-up to the release of his new album. Reports snowballed, and before long it was being reported that he was creating a 'chamber of horrors' at his home, including deformed skulls and a collection of books documenting grotesque medical cases. Another newspaper article wondered if he might commission a cartoon show featuring his pet animals alongside the Elephant Man. The press attention was continuing to come at a price, and it was during the raft of stories about the Elephant Man skeleton that he was first dubbed 'Wacko Jacko' by a British tabloid. Michael might not have been troubled by this but his mother was. Katherine had a stiff word with Michael's manager, Frank DiLeo, who she feared was party to the humiliation of her son. Michael told him not to worry, because his mother did not grasp how the entertainment industry worked. Within a few years of this, he was to regret this as the media dreamt up kooky Jackson stories on an almost weekly basis.

He seemed to not understand – or was in denial over – the origin of this image. 'Wacko Jacko – where'd that come from?' he asked later in an interview with US journalist Barbara Walters. 'Some English tabloid. I have a heart and I have feelings. I feel that when you do that to me. It's not nice. Don't do it. I'm not a "wacko",' he said. Some of the press coverage was accurate though, including the reports in 1987 that he had left the Jehovah's Witnesses movement, to the despair of his mother. 'To my knowledge there's no particular reason,' was the evasive explanation his manager offered. 'He made that decision in his head and that's for him to deal with.' The move was somewhat inevitable as, since the 'Thriller' video episode, singer and religion had been increasingly at odds. Now Michael could pursue the image he wanted, without worrying about the religion. The result of this was clear for all to see on his world tour to promote *Bad*.

Although *Bad* failed to live up the sales of *Thriller*, his world tour saw him break other records. It was the most profitable tour, with Michael trousering $125 million, and the most-attended – 4.4 million people paid to watch him. Across the 123 dates he put on a theatrical show the likes of which had never been seen before in pop. Laser beams, magic tricks and smoke bombs wowed the already hysterical audiences even further. During the song 'Beat It' he would hover above the audience on a crane. His liberation from the grip of the Jehovah's Witnesses movement was clear in the increasingly sexual performances he gave. Michael would regularly grasp his crotch during the concerts in what became a trademark part of his dance routines. He drew 570,000 people in Japan alone, where rather than being dubbed Wacko Jacko he was known as Typhoon Michael.

His first concert of the tour was in Tokyo. When he flew in on Japan Airlines flight 61 a few days ahead of the concert, he had Jimmy Osmond with him, as the Osmond brother was master-minding the business side of the tour. Michael spent the following days rehearsing and visiting the huge Kiddyland toy shop and a local funfair. The media became awash with stories around Michael's presence in the country. It was suggested that he had brought his pet snakes with him and that LaToya was being employed as a decoy by dressing up like him and diverting fans and press. Both stories were untrue, as was the one that suggested Michael was bathing in Perrier water in his suite at Tokyo's Capital Hotel. (This story was a hangover from when he visited London and called in stocks of sparkling water to his hotel room after a strike by water workers led to fears of contaminated supplies.) 'Jacksonmania' was apparent wherever you looked, even a small bric-a-brac store near the hotel was having a '20 per cent off' sale in celebration of his presence in the city.

The concert itself was watched by Chris Heath of *Smash Hits* magazine. 'Just when you think he's only the best dancer in the world,' wrote Heath, 'he sings "Human Nature" and "She's Out of My Life" and sounds strangely like the best singer in the world. At the end of "She's Out of My Life" he wipes away tears so convincingly that you just want to jump on the stage and give him a great big hug.' Heath also observed that Michael fasted from midday Saturday to Monday morning, playing two energetic concerts during his abstinence from food. The audience would not have known this as he put in a series of amazing performances in Japan. There were many thumbs-up for the concert in the British press. *Today* newspaper said, 'No pets, no plastic – just raw sex'; 'Japs go Wacko over raunchy Jacko' said the *News of the World*; 'Magical Michael has his fans in a spell' wrote the *Daily Express* and the *Daily Mirror* simply stated that it had been 'The greatest show on earth'.

In Australia – where he was nicknamed Crocodile Jackson – he was less successful, with some speculating that this was due to the public being put off by the Wacko Jacko news reports. When he arrived in England, he had a royal engagement to keep. Prince Charles and Princess Diana attended the third of the seven shows he put on at London's Wembley Stadium. (Michael had asked his limousine to stop outside Buckingham Palace earlier in the trip, so he could watch the horse-guards march.) Onstage, he could not resist a cheeky, headline-grabbing quip, telling Prince Charles: 'I can give you some dance lessons.' Backstage he presented Diana with black *Bad* tour jackets to pass on to Princes William and Harry. She asked him why he had not sung the song 'Dirty Diana' – his fuming tirade against the groupies of the pop world – and he told her he had removed it from his set list out of respect to her. She laughed and replied that it was one of her favourite Jackson tracks. During another Wembley concert – on 26 August – he stopped proceedings to ask the audience to pray for Elizabeth Taylor, who was unwell. Prior to singing 'I Just Can't Stop Loving You', he said: 'I have a very important message to make. Can I have everybody's attention? A very, very dear friend of mine is very, very sick tonight and the pain that she is experiencing is unbearable. So I ask that everyone in the stadium tonight just bow their heads for five seconds to Elizabeth Taylor…I dedicate this song to Elizabeth Taylor. Thank you very much.' It had been a moment of raw emotion on the stage and melodrama in the wider venue.

Journalist Cynthia Horner, who edited a magazine called *Right On*, was privileged to observe Michael at close quarters backstage at the Wembley concert and in the days around it. She was able to notice how he interacted with fans and described him as 'quiet and humble'. She added: 'However, it may sound strange to say, but people feel energy drawing from him, almost as though he's endowed with superhuman powers. People are usually so struck by him that they cannot even speak. Indeed, Michael weaves a magic spell over his fans.' While in the capital he visited Madame Tussaud's privately with his mother. He also paid visits to the West End's stores one afternoon, popping into an antiques shop and then the giant toy shop Hamley's, where he spent over an hour, purchasing thousands of pounds' worth of presents for a ten-year-old boy he had befriended called Jimmy Safechuck, who accompanied Michael for a part of the tour.

Michael and Safechuck also visited Elstree Studios, where Stephen Spielberg was directing *Indiana Jones and the Last Crusade*, and met Harrison Ford. Michael bought a Rolls Royce car for Safechuck's parents. (Safechuck was later interviewed by the police about his relationship with Michael and insisted the singer never behaved inappropriately towards him.) Many of Michael's team felt uncomfortable over his friendships with children and felt that showering them and their parents with expensive gifts was an especially unwise move. However, with his enormously successful career, who was able to get through to Michael? His family had long despaired of being able to reach him, so what hope did his employees have? The sycophancy that surrounded him at this point is seen in the statement of his former sister-in-law Enid Jackson, in response to his poor ticket sales in Australia. 'He's giving the world a gift – his talent – and in return they crucify him.' The man himself was oozing with ego, too. 'If Elvis is supposed to be the King, what about me?' he asked.

During his UK stay, Michael had appeared on his hotel balcony wrapped in a curtain and waved at the fans gathered below. He also threw notes down to them. One of them, as recounted in *Michael Jackson: The Visual Documentary*, read: 'You all have really proved your loyalty to me. I wish I could truly look you in the eyes and talk to you all, but I'm too shy. It sounds silly but it's true. I truly love all of you very much.' In another he urged fans to ignore the 'strange stories' that were written about him. 'Sometimes I cry,' he wrote, 'but it's fans like you that make me endure.' Hotels would now routinely be mobbed by crowds of hysterical fans wherever Michael travelled and he often played up to them, sometimes with controversial effects.

Reflecting on the *Bad* tour, Michael said: 'For different people, growing up can occur at a different age and now I'm showing the world that I'm the man I always wanted to be.' The tour concluded in Los Angeles. It had proved a huge commercial and creative success, with his enormous profits matched by the astonishing hysteria with which his audiences greeted him. He was approaching Messianic stature in the eyes of many of them. However, while he remained a commercial success, there were hints that an industry backlash might be brewing against Michael. The readers of *Rolling Stone* magazine voted him as the worst artist in most categories in its end of year poll in 1988, including Worst Single, Most Unwelcome Comeback and Worst Dressed Male Singer. Then at the Grammys – where he had won a record eight awards the previous year – he sat stony-faced as he failed to pick up a single gong. He returned to his hotel and cried. As the 1980s drew to an end, 'artist of the decade' polls ran in publications across the world. It was not Michael but Madonna who was emerging at the top of many of these polls. So furious was Michael that his lawyer John Branca was forced to ask MTV to create a special award that he could win at their awards ceremony. They complied and Michael tried his best to appear humble as he was handed the Video Vanguard Artist of the Decade gong by Peter Gabriel.

Disc jockey Jonathan King came out in support of Michael, particularly in regard to the way he had been overlooked at the

ove: The Jackson 5 in 1966, two years
ore they signed with Motown. Michael
s only eight but was already touring
h the band.

ht: A twelve-year-old Michael poses
an early publicity shot, in 1971.

Left: Michael with his mother, Katherine, and father, Joseph Jackson.

Below: The Jackson clan beside the pool at their California home in 197. From left: Jackie, Michael (*foreground*), unidentified, Joseph Katherine, Marlon, LaToya, Randy, Tito, Rebbie and baby daughter, Jermaine and Janet.

ove: Diana Ross with Michael at the
lden Globes in 1973. She was to play a
y role in his life for many years.

ht: A revised line-up and a revised
me: The Jacksons in 1977. Jermaine
d been replaced by Randy after the
up's departure from Motown.
ckwise from top left: Marlon, Jackie,
, Randy and Michael.

Left: Michael sporting the afro hairdo which he and his brothers helped to popularize, 1978.

Below: As the Scarecrow (*second from left*) in *The Wiz*, 1978. Diana Ross played Dorothy.

Left: On a trip to London in 1979, Jackson asked to dress up as Charlie Chaplin and posed for an extraordinary series of photos near where Chaplin was born.

Below: Michael Jackson with record producer Quincy Jones the same year. They had first worked together on *The Wiz*, but their collaboration on *Off the Wall* and *Thriller* took Michael to new levels of superstardom.

Right: The video for 'Billie Jean', the second single from *Thriller*. It was the first video by a black artist to be played on heavy rotation on the new music channel, MTV.

Below: The fourteen-minute film that accompanied the single, 'Thriller', cost $500,000 to make and took music videos to a level that has never been surpassed.

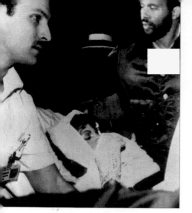

bove: Michael being rushed to ·spital after suffering serious ·rns to his head during a shoot · a Pepsi ad in 1984. The ·cident became a major news ·ent around the world.

·ght: Jackson hysteria was at its ·ak the following year. Here ·chael greets his fans during a ·o to London.

·low: By 1986, tales of Michael's ·d private behaviour were ·eady circulating. Stories of ·chael sleeping in an oxygen tent ·ded to the 'Wacko Jacko' image ·ut it was Michael himself who ·d planted them in the press.

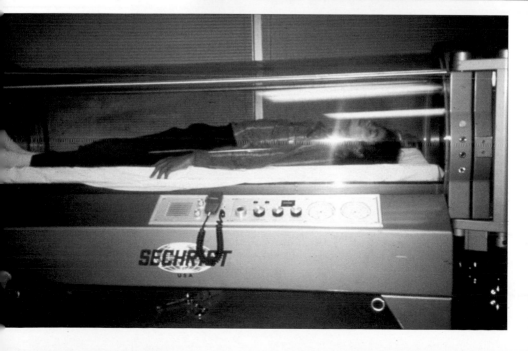

Above: Michael in Liverpool in 1988, on the *Bad* world tour. It remains one of the highest-grossing tour in the history of pop music.

Left: A gravity-defyin scene from the 'Smooth Criminal' vid in *Moonwalker*, Michael's 1988 featur length collection of short films.

Right: The same year, Michael bought Neverland, a ranch in California that was to become his private playground in later years.

1988 Grammys. 'Michael should have swept the board,' he says in *Michael Jackson: The Visual Documentary*. He continued, saying that when Michael performed at the Grammys ceremony he had shamed Sting and Paul Simon, who had won awards that night. 'You should have seen their faces,' he said. 'It was a look of absolute pure, sheer horror. They were transfixed by his real talent and mortified when they compared it to their own stars.' Whether King's speculation over what was going on in Michael's Grammy rivals' mind was accurate or not, his omission from the awards in 1988 was surprising and a difficult moment for Michael, the MTV video award notwithstanding. He was heartened when he learned that a Gallup poll found that members of the royal family were the UK's most loved people overall. Among respondents under the age of twenty-five, however, Michael was the top answer. Soon after this, it was revealed that during 1988 Michael had appeared on the cover of over a hundred major magazines.

Encouraging and significant, but these bits of good news were not enough to fully mask what Michael felt was a growing backlash against him. Behind much of this reverse trend was a fatigue among many music fans over the Wacko Jacko stories of this period. Among these were claims that he was now communicating in 'monkey language' with Bubbles, that the singer Prince had used extra-sensory perception to mentally disturb the chimp, that Michael was claiming to have encountered Jesus Christ while performing on stage and that he wanted to date Princess Diana. None of these stories was true, and their publication deeply upset Michael. However, the story that really shook him was the one claiming that he had fired four members of his team after they tested positive for the HIV virus. The report quoted him speaking with horror at the thought of shaking hands with the employees and also suggested he was having samples of his own blood frozen and transported around with him on the tour.

With his compassionate image so dear to him and with Aids-awareness becoming an ever-more fashionable cause in the entertainment industry, this untrue story was potentially damaging. However, it proved impossible to stem the flow of fabricated media stories about him. In vain had he attempted to wrest control of the situation, first by writing an eccentric note to *People* magazine, including such lines as 'most people don't know me, that is why they write such things in wich [*sic*] most is not true' and 'Animals strike not from malice, but because they want to live, it is the same with those who criticize, they desire our blood, not our pain.' It hardly helped promote an image of Michael as a balanced man.

His second move was to publish his autobiography, *Moonwalk*. Here, he attempted to put across the truth of his life and career. 'People often ask me what I'm like,' he wrote in its concluding pages. 'I hope this book will answer some of those questions.' However, on the book's publication in 1988, much of the media's attention focused on the passages in which he – lightly, it must be said – criticized his father for his excessive punishment of Michael and his brothers when they were children. In the wake of the reports which extracted these passages, Michael rang his father to apologize, and claimed that much of the book had been 'ghost-written' by someone else. Such arrangements are commonplace in celebrity autobiographies, and he reportedly went through several such collaborators before being happy with the finished product, but it seems unlikely that – whatever his involvement in the writing of it – Michael would have allowed the manuscript to be published without his approval.

It was released in April 1988, after maximum security had surrounded its printing and distribution to avoid early leaks. Stories about this secrecy became a plank of the book's promotional campaign, which publishers Doubleday felt was essential because, as one employee told the *New York Times*, they feared Michael's typical fan 'does not necessarily run to bookstores often'. Relatives of Doubleday staff were used to deliver the book to the printers, rather than using an outside courier as was usual. Once *Moonwalk* arrived at the printing plant in Fairfield, Pennsylvania it was given the codename Neil Armstrong – the name of the first man to walk on the moon. It went to number one in the book charts of the *New York Times*, *Los Angeles Times* and *The Times* (UK) and quickly sold over half a million copies around the world. Remarkably, it was later adapted into a forty-seven-page text book to help Japanese high school students learn the English language.

None of which was enough to stem the flow of tabloid stories about Michael. If anything, the success of the book merely reconfirmed his popularity in the eyes of tabloid newspaper editors and maintained his status as their number-one target. If he had hoped to introduce a sane image of himself to the public with *Moonwalk*, he failed. As reviewer Ken Tucker wrote in the *New York Times*, 'For as much as his book reveals of his connection to the everyday world, he might as well be walking on the moon.' Michael was perhaps becoming resigned to his Wacko Jacko image, because his behaviour continued to be outlandish to say the least. A prime example of this was the way he decorated a ranch he had recently bought in Santa Ynez in California. Michael had first visited the property and land, called Sycamore Ranch, when he rented it to stay in while he and Paul McCartney shot the promotional video for 'Say Say Say'. Indeed, it was Michael's admiration of McCartney's own home that attracted him to the idea of purchasing a property as grand as Sycamore. He wanted to show guests – and the world – how successful he was and felt that buying a huge ranch would be the best way of doing it. He contacted the owner, William Bone, and arranged to tour the land in style: the pair were transported by horse and carriage around the grounds.

Michael became obsessed with obtaining the ranch and harassed his lawyer Branca into closing the deal. Bone was asking for approximately $30 million, Michael was offering just $17 million – no wonder the negotiations were taking their time. Finally the deal was closed at Michael's price, but media reports claimed that he had paid closer to $28 million. Michael's family were surprised that he was finally leaving the family home, a two-acre estate at 4621 Hayvenhurst in Encino, California. They had moved there in 1971, the day after Katherine turned forty-one. The property was less than an hour's drive from Hollywood and the estate had its own security gate and an outbuilding for the staff. Michael's parents and siblings were also a little hurt that he neither informed them of his purchase of the ranch, nor invited them to the subsequent housewarming bash.

Here, perhaps, he was drawing another line in the sand between him and the influence of his father. Katherine, though, was caught up in this dispute and was very upset by how Michael handled his move. It must have been a difficult move for Michael too. In 1983 he said, 'I'd die of loneliness if I ever moved out.' But move out he did and nobody, apart from Michael himself, could have predicted what he had in mind for the land he had just bought.

Successful, rich people have often bought grand properties and large areas of land to celebrate their wealth. Former presidents such as Ronald Reagan and George Bush Sr built ranches which hark back to their political heydays. George Lucas built Skywalker Ranch in California. The *Star Wars* director's ranch includes a farm, vineyards, a man-made Lake Ewok and numerous private cinemas. It even has its own fire station. This was modest and restrained, though, compared to the way Michael would develop his property, renamed Neverland, in the years to come. In an interview on CNN after Michael's death, Jermaine looked around the ranch, smiled and told Larry King: 'This is his creation. This is his wonder and his joy, his happiness, his peace.' However, author Chris Ayers, who visited Neverland in the 1990s, was less complimentary. He described Neverland as being akin to 'a private island owned by some whacked-out Third World dictator'.

It was certainly a garish place once Michael had put his personal stamp on it. Visitors would pull up to a pair of extravagant golden gates in which a 'royal' Jackson crest and a silhouette of Peter Pan had been included. 'Once upon a time,' read the text emblazoned on the gates which would open to reveal a spectacular view of Neverland. The driveways included a statue of Michael and were lined with numerous metal sculptures of children, one of them a naked boy. Neverland had its own zoo which housed a menagerie of animals including elephants, tigers, exotic snakes and a giraffe. Michael lived in a five-bedroom house decorated with – among other things – oil paintings of Elizabeth Taylor. The property included a giant kitchen and a private cinema, in which stood a model of the singer. A playroom was built, its door-knobs shaped like miniature basketballs.

A train track circled the ranch, on which a small red steam train ran, touring the grounds. Golf carts were also available for the same purpose. On a hill stood a train station which mimicked one Michael had seen at Disneyland, complete with an enormous floral clock. 'Neverland' was spelt out in yellow flowers and a waxwork elderly couple sat on the station bench. There was a station snack bar with a spiral staircase. A Walt Disney soundtrack was perpetually piped out of fake rocks – his own tunes were never thus broadcast at the ranch. Visitors who hopped aboard the train would have been astonished by what they saw. Michael had commissioned a fairground which was home to a number of rides including a roller coaster designed especially for children, a merry-go-round, bumper cars and a Ferris wheel. There was also a computer-games arcade and a Native American village complete with wigwams. An outdoor banquet table was placed under a tree. Neverland had its own private security team of forty guards who would prowl the grounds. Michael even had a codename used by the staff at Neverland – Silver Fox.

This was celebrity indulgence gone wild. The childlike theme raised some eyebrows. Most famous men who built ranches stuck to decidedly macho themes, but Michael built Neverland as a gentle, childish affair. At first, the childlike name of the property and the way he had decorated it was seen as nothing more sinister than Michael indulging his Peter Pan side. He was a kid who had never grown up and so wanted to live in a childlike home. In due course, a more sinister interpretation would be put on his home by some. In the meantime, though, Neverland was more than a home to Michael. It was a canvas onto which he could project his imagination, hopes and dreams. This was how he saw the world in his mind and how he wanted the world to look and be. Forget reading *Moonwalk*, if you really wanted to understand what made Michael Jackson tick then you could not have done better than to visit Neverland in its heyday.

None of it came cheap, of course, and while Neverland was being built, Michael began to complain loudly about his financial situation. His bank balance had not been helped by the making of *Moonwalker*, a self-indulgent, semi-autobiographical movie that Michael spent $27 million making. 'From the imagination of Michael Jackson comes a movie like no other,' boasted the film's promotional strap line. It was a collection of short films which loosely told the story of his life. In one he poked fun at his public image, boogieing with the skeleton of the Elephant Man. Despite the huge budget for the film it was never released to cinemas in America after negotiations broke down. In the end it was released on video in January 1989, two years after its planned release date. It sold healthily and he recouped his massive investment, turning a small profit. All the same, Michael nearly had his fingers burned financially and – given his stated dream of having a future in Hollywood – creatively with this project and in its wake he vowed to rein in his indulgent spending on such ventures.

Little could he know that in just a few years he would hand over a small fortune to a family to buy their silence...

CHAPTER FOUR

It should not be forgotten that Michael was a money-making machine at his peak and beyond. In March 1991 he signed a new deal with Sony Corp. It was a record-breaking deal: estimates vary from $50 million to $65 million. Michael was to spend sixteen months recording his next album, with much of the work taking place at Record One studios in Los Angeles. This time he worked with a new producer – Teddy Riley – having parted company professionally with Quincy Jones after the making of *Bad*. Riley recalls how Michael craved and pushed for both originality and perfection. 'He always pushed me to be different and innovative and strong. He was demanding and we'd work on songs for a long time; we always had to get the mix right.' Eventually, Jones was called so he could hear the mixes. Michael felt that only with the nod of approval from his former producer could he finally release the mixes to the record company. Jones was, Riley says, Michael's 'quality controller'. One plan for the album that never materialized was a duet with Madonna. During the spring of 1991 he had been photographed with her a number of times, prompting rumours of a romance. However, they were actually merely discussing a (never to happen) duet. The pair did, though, spark fury among followers of an Islamic party in Pakistan when they announced interest in co-headlining a show in the province.

The hard work paid off as another astoundingly good Michael Jackson album hit the shops on 26 November 1991. *Dangerous* opened with 'Jam', which Michael had co-written with Riley, Bruce Swedien and Rene Moore. It was an obvious opener for an album and went on to replace 'Wanna Be Startin' Somethin'' as the opener for live sets. Another stand-out song was 'Remember the Time', which he co-wrote with Riley after revealing the first time he met future wife Debbie Rowe. It reached number three in the UK. The very title of the track 'In the Closet' raised eyebrows in many quarters. However, it was not about homosexuality, nor about the closet in which Joseph had hidden his guitar back on Jackson Street. Instead it was about any lovers who were forced to keep their romance secret. *Dangerous* closed with a song of the same name. Michael had co-written the track with Bill Bottrell and Teddy Riley after the pair picked up on some basic melodies hummed by Michael and developed them in the studio. It was a great end to the album and was originally selected to be an unprecedented tenth single to be lifted from the album, before the intervention of a boy by the name of Jordan Chandler put paid to that plan.

In the meantime, *Dangerous* was another hotly anticipated album. Six days prior to its release, 30,000 copies of it had been stolen by armed robbers at Los Angeles airport. On its release it went straight to number one in the US and UK. It was also a critical success. *Rolling Stone* reviewer Alan Light said that the album at times 'Rises to the impossible challenge set by *Thriller*, the commercial and artistic juggernaut that will always loom over Michael Jackson's work. At his best, then and now, the dancer and the dance come together and reveal a man, no longer a man-child, confronting his well-publicized demons and achieving transcendence through performance.' David Browne, of *Entertainment Weekly*, was less impressed, writing that 'even the most acute studio skills can't compensate for the hole-in-the-soul that haunts the album'. The *Chicago Tribune*, meanwhile, accused the King of Pop of 'playing it safe'. John Pareless of the *New York Times* had a related criticism: 'The problem with *Dangerous* isn't that Jackson is "different"; it's that *Dangerous* keeps too much of his weirdness in the closet.'

The album had been trailed by one of Michael's most memorable singles: 'Black or White'. Written by Michael (with Bill Bottrell adding the words for the rap segment) it was a plea for racial harmony which drew comparisons with *Thriller*'s 'Beat It', thanks to its lively rock guitar. The theme of the song reflected a longstanding Jackson value: as far back as the 1970s he had read about how the colours of peacocks' wings integrate when the bird is in love, and wanted to bring this feeling of unity and love into his work. He had been extra-vigilant with security around the recording, sending two bodyguards (at a cost of nearly £10,000) to accompany the master tape of the song on a Concorde flight from America to London. Once released, it became the first single by an American artist to enter the UK singles chart at number one since Elvis Presley soared straight to the top in 1960 with 'It's Now or Never'. The video caused controversy for the scene in which Michael smashes a car up and breaks windows. 'It upsets me to think "Black or White" could influence any child or adult to destructive behaviour, either sexual or violent,' said Michael in a statement and the segment was removed. None of this stopped it from being a hit around the world and it is one of the catchiest songs of Michael's entire career.

As well as thrilling the public, Michael was continuing to influence other artists. Justin Timberlake is a lifelong fan and when the former 'N Sync singer was offered an opportunity to meet Michael in 1991 he jumped at the chance. While staying at the Four Seasons hotel on East 57th street in Manhattan, Michael sent for Timberlake and was excited to meet the young rising solo star. However, according to Taraborrelli, when he learned that Timberlake would be bringing his girlfriend, pop star Britney Spears, to the meeting he was furious and wondered whether she could be excluded at the last moment. In the end both Timberlake and Spears came to Michael's suite and by the time they had finished showering him with praise and recounting how profoundly he had influenced them Michael had forgotten his initial ire at Spears' presence.

When he toured the globe to promote *Dangerous*, he donated profits from the sixty-seven-concert tour to a new charitable venture he had formed – the Heal the World Foundation, which was named after the *Dangerous* track 'Heal the World'. As well as sending funds around the world to aid children affected by conflict, disease and poverty, it paid for underprivileged children to come to Neverland. He was soon planning a World Congress of Children, which would unite kids from a hundred different countries. The Dangerous tour was memorable mostly for the 'rocket man finale' stunt that closed each show. Michael would – it appeared to audiences – strap a rocket belt onto his body and fly right out of the open-air venue. This role was actually performed by a body double but all the same it was an eye-catching and headline-grabbing stunt, straight from the Jackson textbook of pop and public relations wizardry.

Although *Dangerous* was a great and successful album, it could be said that he was currently doing his best work not in the studio but on the stage. Two live performances by Michael in the early 1990s summed up the contrasts and complexities of his life. The first came at the Soul Train Awards in March 1993. He was there to sing 'Remember the Time', the second single to be lifted from *Dangerous*. He would also receive an award for both the single and the album. He appeared at the ceremony in a wheelchair and word was put about that he had twisted his ankle during the rehearsals. His performance in the chair, with his dance troupe jiving around him, was memorable to say the least. The press certainly reported it widely, putting him back in the headlines. The next day he was walking perfectly normally, leading many to conclude the wheelchair had been unnecessary and merely another headline-grabbing trick. However, the day after that he appeared at an American film industry dinner walking on crutches.

The Soul Train Awards performance was memorable for the wrong reasons but his half-time show at the Super Bowl will live on in the memory for all the right ones. This was a key, iconic moment in his life and also in the history of the NFL event itself, which was never the same after Michael rocked it in 1993. Prior to Michael's appearance it had struggled to attract big-name stars, but in the wake of his epochal performance it pulled in the likes of Diana Ross, Stevie Wonder, Christina Aguilera, Aerosmith, U2,

Shania Twain, The Rolling Stones, Prince and Bruce Springsteen. For Michael had noted something no top act had before: the Super Bowl was broadcast to more than a hundred countries where a certain type of viewer dominated. 'We talked to him about the blue-collar football fan that might not otherwise be a Michael Jackson fan and about how he could build a new fan base,' said Arlen Kantarian, who produced the half-time performance. 'He got that…he was very sharp and very shy.'

He was anything but shy on the day. Fireworks exploded as he was fired onto the stage. He landed and stood completely still, like a statue. Dressed in gold and black and wearing sunglasses, he cut an incredible figure. The audience responded wildly, cheering, screaming and willing him to launch into his performance. On and on he stood there, for two tension-building minutes. It is hard to imagine another artist getting away with such indulgence. Michael did more than get away with it – the crowd loved it. Finally, the music kicked in and he began to dance. He performed 'Jam', 'Billie Jean', 'Black or White' and 'Heal the World'. (He had originally insisted that he just sing new tracks, but eventually agreed to include 'Billie Jean'.) A hundreds-strong choir and thousands of children joined him for the closing song of the set which was the talk of the nation for days afterwards. In those days, Michael did not do anything half-heartedly.

Broadcasters NBC reported higher viewing figures for the twenty-minute half-time set than it had for the first half of the tie between the Dallas Cowboys and the Buffalo Bills. Michael too benefited from his energetic performance being beamed into homes across the globe: 'Dangerous' shot back up the charts, rising ninety places in the wake of his Super Bowl set which was watched by 120 million people. He launched a Michael Jackson chocolate bar in America, which earned him an estimated £1 million in its first month on sale. These were good days for Michael: little could he have known the nightmare that was just around the corner for him. In the meantime, though, he wallowed in his status as a living legend. He was anointed as that at the Grammy awards the following month. It was to be Michael's final major public engagement before his world changed for ever. He arrived at the ceremony with Brooke Shields on his arm and walked away carrying the Living Legend award which had been presented to him by his sister Janet. Michael joked that he hoped this would end rumours that he and Janet were the same person.

As we have seen, as the 1980s drew to an end Michael was feeling snubbed by the numerous polls which looked back over the decade in pop music and failed to sufficiently recognize his contribution. Soon, though, his brilliance as a pop legend was being reflected by fresh awards and plaudits. In 1992, he had returned to the White House where President Reagan's successor, George H. W. Bush, had another honour lined up for him – the Point of Light Ambassador award. Praising Michael for building a 'tremendous following', he called the singer a 'leading light of the world' and a role model for young black men. He was a role model for people of all colours but some of his fans were proving *far* too enthralled by him. In July 1992 a fan called Eric Herminie stood on a ledge some 120 feet above the pavement opposite Michael's hotel in London and threatened to jump to his certain death unless the singer spoke to him. Michael did so by telephone and also waved to the fan.

Thankfully Herminie agreed to step down and was arrested for breach of peace.

Having been singled out by one superpower in the form of George Bush and America, Michael was soon distinguishing himself in the capital of the other. Michael was the first Western pop star to perform in Russia after the end of the Soviet era. He arrived in Moscow in 1993 and caused the sort of hysteria he sparked anywhere else in the world. He performed at the Luzhniki Open Arena in Moscow. 'It was delayed for three or four hours,' radio producer Vladimir Ivanenko told CNN. 'It was a very rainy day in Moscow that evening and it was an open air concert. It was so wet that his assistants had to sweep the stage all the time during the songs. For people in Russia it was something extraordinary. Everyone was excited that Michael Jackson was in Russia. The quality of the show and sound was shocking for people. He put on quite a show for them. It was incomparable to anything they had ever seen.' He added: 'For Russians, America was like another planet and Michael Jackson was the king of that planet...[He] was seen as the face of the crazy American life.' (This was not his first 'Cold War moment'. He had caused bedlam at the Berlin Wall in 1988 when thousands of East Germans had gathered to try to hear his performance and after he performed in Romania in 1992, a local politician said the concert was 'worth ten years of diplomacy with the West'.)

Michael's international fame was boosted yet further when he decided to give his first in-depth television interview for nearly fourteen years to broadcasting legend Oprah Winfrey – the chat was later to be named 'the TV mega event of the year' by *People* magazine. That interview took place in February 1993, just two days after he had appeared on the cover of *Jet* magazine alongside Winfrey. The interviewer – and the world at large – had lots of questions for Michael. All the same, it was hardly an overly probing quiz, yet Michael appeared very uncomfortable at times. Not least so when the conversation turned to his love life. This was a topic that had eluded the attentions of even the most curious and intrusive media. He was asked who, if anyone, he had dated. 'Well, right now it's Brooke Shields,' he replied. 'Well, we try not to be everywhere, go everywhere, it's mostly at home. She'll come over, I'll go to her house, because I don't like going out in public.' Winfrey then asked him whether or not he was a virgin. 'How could you ask me that question?' said an embarrassed Michael who, when pressed, would only respond that he was 'a gentleman'.

Discussion then turned to the childlike theme Michael had built Neverland around. Winfrey asked him whether he had designed it thus for his own benefit, or for the benefit of 'all the children you entertain here'. He replied that it was for both. As the conversation went on it became – particularly in retrospect – ever more unfortunate. Michael boasted of 'entertaining' children suffering from cancer at Neverland. 'I love to do things for children and I try to imitate Jesus,' he continued. 'I am not saying I am Jesus, I'm not saying that.' He also said he had had plastic surgery, but 'very, very little'. He suggested – seemingly oblivious of his unwise choice of word – that those 'nosey' enough to be interested in his plastic surgery should read his autobiography, *Moonwalk*. Elizabeth Taylor joined the interview for one segment, saying of Michael: 'He is the least weird man I have ever known.'

Taylor's assessment of him confused viewers and – if anything – painted an even weirder picture of Michael and his existence. The interview might not have stemmed suspicion that Michael was an oddball, but it certainly helped maintain his pre-eminent level of fame. Again, Michael capitalized commercially from this moment of television, watched by over 90 million Americans and many more around the world. *Dangerous* went back into the top ten in the wake of its broadcasting. However, he was about to have his world rocked by an enormous scandal. The questions that Winfrey asked Michael had made him uncomfortable at times. However, this was nothing compared to the level of scrutiny he was about to encounter as he stood in front of the jury of the world and faced a very painful allegation about his private life.

* * *

As previously mentioned, Jordan Chandler reportedly first came to Michael's attention in 1984 as he recuperated from the Pepsi advertisement accident and replied to Chandler's fan mail, telling him he was a 'beautiful young boy'. Five years later Michael sent free tickets for the boy and his parents to attend a concert by him in Los Angeles. The pair did not meet properly until May 1992, when the firm managed by Chandler's stepfather David Schwartz was by chance called upon to rent a car to Michael, whose jeep had just broken down on Wilshire Boulevard in Beverly Hills. Jordan and his mother June were called to the scene and the boy finally got to meet one of his biggest idols. June passed the family's telephone number to Michael and suggested he stay in touch with her and Jordan. Imagine Jordan's surprise when the King of Pop agreed to do just that, allegedly saying, 'Oh boy' as he tucked the number away in his pocket.

Jordan returned home excited by the meeting and the prospect of a friendship with perhaps the most famous man on the planet. It was to be another week until he heard from Michael, who telephoned for a chat. He asked Jordan what he liked doing, and the boy mentioned computer games. Michael immediately invited the twelve-year-old to his flat in Century City, California where he had many arcade games. June declined Jordan permission to go, urging him to concentrate on his schoolwork. Michael continued to phone the boy, staying in touch regularly throughout his *Dangerous* tour. During these telephone conversations Michael became obsessed with Jordan and wooed the boy with descriptions of his Neverland ranch, his charity work and celebrity fans. What boy of twelve would not have been intoxicated by this talk and by the attention of his pop hero? When Michael returned to Neverland mid-tour he was once more on the phone to Jordan, telling him how great the ranch was and that if only the boy were with him, it would be 'absolutely perfect'.

In February 1993, Jordan finally visited Neverland, along with his mother June and half-sister Lily. They had a dream day touring the ranch, playing games and watching yet-to-be-released Hollywood films in Michael's private cinema. They even visited a toy shop where the singer told them they could have whatever they wanted. Neither Jordan nor Lily needed any encouragement and duly grabbed thousands of dollars' worth of toys from the shelves of the shop. In the evening they returned to Neverland and took a trip on the Ferris wheel. While they sat looking out over the ranch, bathed in moonlight, Michael confided that he felt his life had a gaping hole in it. 'The things I really want in my life I don't have,' he mourned. Jordan was moved by this. He embraced Michael and said, 'You have us now.'

The following morning, Jordan and his family left the ranch. Michael had made the boy feel the centre of his world during the weekend and promised to see him again soon. However, when the pair next met the following weekend, Michael had another boy in tow. Brett Barnes was eleven years old and another of Michael's friends. When Jordan climbed into Michael's limousine that weekend he found Barnes sitting on Michael's lap and the pair locked in a largely impenetrable conversation. Barnes's possessions were taken to Michael's room at Neverland while Jordan and his family were ushered to outside buildings. The message was clear: the way to Michael's heart was to get as close as possible to him physically.

He continued to be in touch with both boys. He took Jordan and his family to his property on Wilshire Boulevard and then to Las Vegas. It was here that Michael's relationship with the boy took on a new, sinister dimension. After June and Lily had gone to bed, Michael and Jordan watched the 1973 adult horror film *The Exorcist*. As the scary film depicting the demonic possession of a young girl played out, twelve-year-old Jordan became increasingly terrified. Michael could have predicted this reaction, because as he said in an interview in 1983, 'I can't sleep after watching [a horror movie], it just scares me.' That night Jordan stayed in Michael's bed. When his mother discovered this the following morning she was quite naturally horrified and ordered her son to never sleep with Michael again. She confronted Michael, too. The singer burst into tears during their conversation and June was eventually placated. Michael urged her to trust him and she said she would. He presented her with a diamond bracelet the following day. It was worth many thousands of dollars. A month later when the family returned for another visit to Neverland, Michael and Jordan once more shared a bed, with mannequin figures placed outside the bedroom to 'guard them' from ghosts.

Jordan's father Evan was far from impressed with this behaviour. He was stunned by his ex-wife's descriptions of their visits to Neverland and gave her reassurances short shrift. As well as his natural concern about a man in his thirties sharing a bed with his pre-teen son, Evan also felt that Michael was rivalling his paternal role. The holidays, the expensive gifts – one of them the exact same model of computer that Evan had planned to buy his son – were all making him restless with worry. With good reason, as the relationship between the thirty-four-year-old megastar and the twelve-year-old boy became increasingly strange. They had furtive conversations and Michael would often burst into tears when they parted. They even created a manifesto of secret laws for Jordan to live by. Among these were 'No wenches, bitches, heifers or hos', 'Live with me in Neverland forever' and 'Never grow up'. This blend of controlling paranoia and thinly veiled misogyny suggested Michael was terrified of losing his grip on Jordan as he entered his teenage years.

Michael took Jordan, his mother and half-sister to Monaco for the World Music Awards where he was to receive gongs in three categories. Again, he was wooing the boy, who was his guest of honour, in his expensive hotel suite and at the ceremony itself, where Jordan sat on the singer's lap. While staying in the hotel, a book later claimed, their relationship became explicitly sexual as Jordan prepared to take a bath. 'While I was taking off my shirt Michael took me in his arms and began to kiss me,' Jordan is quoted as saying in Victor M. Gutierrez's book *Michael Jackson Was My Lover: The Secret Diary of Jordan Chandler*, later serialized in the *News of the World* Sunday newspaper. 'Michael finished taking off my shirt. When I was left only in my underwear he pulled them down and took them off with his teeth. Finally, we kissed on the mouth. Michael looked at me and told me it had been fantastic.' The singer added, Jordan said, that the pair were destined to be a couple.

According to the same book, Michael admitted to Jordan that he was not the first underage boy the singer had sexual encounters with and used manipulative means to ensnare Jordan into a similar set-up. Jordan recalled: 'Michael said things like "I've had several sexual encounters with another boy. I still do. We have a very good time." Michael said if I wouldn't do those things with him he'd take it as "perhaps Jordy doesn't love me as much as the other boy loves me".' All of these details – later contested by Michael – were hidden from Jordan's family. However, their suspicions were rising. Jordan – previously a well-liked boy at school – was losing touch with his school friends. Finally, his father decided to confront the singer about his bizarre and intense relationship with his son.

After paying a surprise visit to his ex-wife's home while Michael was there, Evan took the singer to one side and asked him what precisely was 'the nature' of his relationship with his son. 'It's cosmic,' replied Michael after some prevarication and mumbling. Unsatisfied with this vague response, Evan went to the core of his concern. 'Look, are you having sex with my son,' he asked Michael. The singer was stunned and giggled with nerves. 'My God, I can't believe you would ask me that,' he replied. Despite Michael's failure to deny that anything improper was occurring, Evan was seemingly at least in part reassured by this encounter. He was soon suggesting that Michael come and stay with Jordan at his house and even proposed building an extension onto the property, so he could stay in it. In the coming weeks Jordan's father and Michael built up a rapport. However, able to observe Jordan and Michael at close range, Evan became more worried and quizzed Michael further. The singer took to avoiding Evan whenever possible, while continuing his relationship with his son.

Finally, Evan had had enough. He applied for a court order banning Michael from any contact with his son. In the same document he took a swipe at his ex-wife, suggesting she had permitted the relationship to continue after receiving presents, money and paid-for holidays from the singer. Relations between June and her ex-husband were crumbling and the person suffering most was Jordan himself. Soon, June's current husband David intervened. It was his chance meeting with Michael that had led to Jordan and Michael's relationship, so perhaps he felt an added sense of responsibility. He secretly recorded a telephone conversation with Evan. The father's anger is clear in the transcripts of the call, but he does not mention at any point a suspicion that there was a sexual dimension in his son and Michael's relationship. Furthermore, when David asked Evan how his plan to 'destroy

Jackson forever' would help his son's state of mind, he stormed: 'That's irrelevant to me.' When Michael was warned of Evan's fighting talk – 'It will be a massacre if I don't get what I want' – he initially shrugged it off, but when he heard the actual recording and heard the fury in Evan's voice, he appointed a legal team to deal with the matter.

One lawyer in that team was Anthony Pellicano, a formidable legal talent. Alongside him was Bert Fields, an equally imposing force. Pellicano interviewed Jordan and recalled that after an hour of the boy denying that anything improper occurred between himself and Michael, he became ever more certain of his client's innocence. Meanwhile, Fields was negotiating with Evan's lawyer Barry Rothman. They agreed that Evan – who was still friendly with Michael – could have a week's custody of his son. However, June failed to show up with Jordan at the agreed time. Soon the lawyers were on the phone to Michael, explaining how unwise it was to prevent the custody week going ahead. When June witnessed Michael's fuming argument with his lawyers she decided to turn Jordan over to his father after all. Michael was devastated and felt he had been betrayed. She felt vindicated in her decision when she subsequently spoke with two police detectives who said they strongly believed Michael to be a paedophile. The tide was beginning to turn and it was about to turn even further. Evan, who was a practising dentist, interviewed his son under the influence of a drug called sodium amytal, which is thought to increase suggestibility and has also been connected with prompting 'false memory syndrome'. Under this questioning, Jordan answered that yes, Michael had touched his genitals.

Michael was only to meet Evan once more – at a tense summit on 4 August 1993 arranged by the rival legal teams. The behaviour of Michael and Jordan did not follow the pattern many would expect had the singer sexually abused the boy. They ran into each other's arms and embraced. When Evan flung accusations at Michael, Jordan did not back them up. Furthermore, as Pellicano observed, Evan was in the same room as a man he purportedly believed had sexually molested his son. 'If I had got so close [to someone he believed had molested his child],' the lawyer is quoted as saying, 'I would be on death row right now.' Instead, Evan demanded Michael take a lie detector test and left the room vowing, 'I'm going to ruin you.'

Soon, Evan named a sum that would convince him not to pursue legal action. It was $20 million. Offers and counter-offers were then exchanged between the parties, mostly involving funding for film production. (Evan and his son had been involved in the making of a film before meeting Michael and had ambitions to make more.) Negotiations soon broke down and the entire story – which had thus far been proceeding in secret – was imminently to enter the public domain. Michael's career as a pop superstar was about to be dealt a considerable blow. Jordan had, at his father's behest, a three-hour meeting with a psychiatrist during which he gave a fulsome account of a history of sexual abuse from Michael. He also declared that he wanted to remain in the custody of his father, rather than returning to his mother. June, on hearing of the interview, had her doubts over the veracity of what her son had said. It was too late, though, to stop the matter being turned over to the police and with them, the media.

* * *

On 17 August, the Los Angeles Police Department officially opened a criminal investigation into the allegations of sexual abuse made against Michael Jackson by Jordan Chandler. With the focus of the allegations in Asia on the second leg of his *Dangerous* tour, Neverland ranch was searched by the police. J. Randy Taraborrelli alleges that in the days leading up to the search Michael's staff had emptied the ranch of lots of items which might have seemed incriminating, among them a photograph of child actor Macaualy Culkin in his underwear. The *Home Alone* actor had been a friend of Michael's for some time, even holidaying with him in Bermuda. When police arrived with a locksmith to open the property's numerous doors, they quickly concluded that a clean-up operation had occurred. All the same, they gathered pieces of evidence to take away and examine. Michael had left some prankish traps around the place too, including a human-sized safe which took police hours to get open. Once they had they saw it contained nothing but a case – which they eventually prized open to find nothing but the combination for the safe.

Six days later, word began to leak to the media that Michael was under investigation over some very serious charges. A television station reported the search and the *New York Post* picked this up and ran it under the headline 'Peter Pan Or Pervert?' Pellicano took control, formally announcing the investigation and its nature. He said the allegations were entirely false and had surfaced after Evan's attempts to get Michael to fund some cinematic projects were refused. It was 'an extortion attempt' he told reporters. In a statement issued via lawyer Howard Weitzman, Michael painted a picture of quiet self-belief, confidence in the legal system and business as normal on the road. 'My representatives have continuously kept me aware of what is taking place in California. I appreciate the remarks of Chief Willie Williams of our Los Angeles Police Department. I am confident the department will conduct a fair and thorough investigation and its results will demonstrate that there was no wrongdoing on my part. I intend to continue with my world tour, and look forward to seeing you all in the scheduled cities. I am grateful for the overwhelming support of my fans throughout the world. I love you all. Thank you, Michael.' He would need all the help he could get – the editor of one tabloid newspaper in the US declared the Chandler investigation 'the biggest story since [Elvis] Presley's death'.

A public relations campaign was launched to defend Michael from the inevitable avalanche of lurid headlines and fevered media speculation. LaToya Jackson's husband and manager Jack Gordon told *USA Today* that the allegations were entirely false. 'He really loves children,' said Gordon. 'He would never harm a child.' Brett Barnes and Wade Robson, two of the boys whom Michael had befriended in recent times, were also wheeled in front of the cameras and reporters to protest their hero and friend's innocence. 'He kisses you like you kiss your mother,' said Barnes. 'It's not unusual for him to hug, kiss and nuzzle up to you, and stuff.' Wade added: 'Sure I slept with him on dozens of occasions but the bed was huge.' While both insisted nothing sexual or abusive had occurred, their words were far from ideal in painting Michael as an innocent man in the court of public opinion. However, by and large Michael's fans believed his side of the story. On 27 August he performed in front of an audience of 70,000 in Bangkok, Thailand, and throughout the night they chanted in support of him and waved banners reading 'I Love You' and other positive slogans. Two days later he celebrated his thirty-fifth birthday and the 47,000 fans attending his concert in Singapore sang 'Happy Birthday' to him. On the same day, English fans protested in Piccadilly Circus against what they called the 'Trial by Tabloid' that Michael was facing. (This was not the first time British fans had rallied in his support: in July 1992 they pelted a *Daily Mirror* photographer with horse manure after he took what they deemed an intrusive photograph of their hero.) When Pepsi announced that they were cancelling their business relationship with Michael, his fans arranged a boycott of the drink. Two months later their rivals Coca-Cola announced a 20 per cent increase in sales and thus had the last laugh after poking fun at Michael's cancellation of a concert due to dehydration with an advertisement that read: 'Dehydrated? There's Always Coca-Cola.'

On 30 August, the Jackson family held a press conference in which they clearly stated their belief in Michael's innocence and offered their full support. Their statement read that they wanted to 'take this opportunity, when our family has come together in unity and harmony, to convey our love and unfailing support for Michael...It is our unequivocal belief that Michael has been made the victim of a cruel and obvious attempt to take advantage of his fame and success. We know, as does the whole world, that he has dedicated his life to providing happiness for young people everywhere. We are confident that his dignity and humanity will prevail.' The press conference had been pre-planned, to announce a TV show entitled *The Jackson Family Honours* which had been Jermaine's idea. Michael was comforted when he learned of what his family had said in support of him. However, when they arrived in Asia to offer their love and support in person he refused to see them and told his publicist to turn them away.

That same evening he collapsed just seconds before his concert in Singapore was due to start. He had a migraine and the performance had to be cancelled. He had a brain scan the following day and issued a statement apologizing to fans. 'I was suddenly taken ill last night, and I am sorry for the cancellation of my performance…Thank you for your continued support and understanding. I love you all. Thank you.' When he was unable to visit the Singapore Zoo, six monkeys were driven to Michael's hotel so he could 'meet' them there. Meanwhile, the Chandler camp hired a well-known Los Angeles lawyer called Gloria Allred, but within a matter of days she had walked out on the case and would not reveal why she had quit. June's lawyer, Michael Freeman, also resigned, saying he felt that Evan was 'not a genuine person' and that Michael had been 'wrongly accused'.

In September, LaToya appeared on the *Today* show, an American television programme. Although she said she supported her brother 'one thousand per cent', she also said of the allegations made against him 'but we don't really know'. If she had been attempting to offer help to Michael her words had the exact opposite effect. A few months later she would make his public standing even worse. Elizabeth Taylor also waded in to offer assistance. She flew to Asia to join Michael and firmly told reporters that the allegations were false and an extortion attempt. Once back in America she attempted to wrestle control of the case, advising Michael by telephone who to hire and who to fire as his representatives. Michael became more and more terrified and traumatized by the allegations. In November he cancelled the remainder of his *Dangerous* tour and announced that he had become dependent on painkillers, due to the stress of the allegations. Among those he was taking were codeine, Demerol and Percodan. He also became hooked on tranquilizing drugs such as Valium. There then followed a game of hide and seek, in which the media tried to guess where Michael was staying and he kept them guessing.

One person who knew very well where the megastar was staying was Lisa Marie Presley. As we have seen, he first met her when The Jacksons appeared in Las Vegas in the 1970s, when her legendary father Elvis brought her to one of the shows. If anyone outside the family could understand Michael's childhood and life in general it was the daughter of Elvis Presley. Not only had she enjoyed a strange upbringing – showered with gifts, including a fur coat as a five-year-old – she had also witnessed at first hand the effect of superstardom on her father. Elvis Presley died when she was just nine years old, with Lisa Marie finding her father's dead body. She and Michael met again at the start of 1993, when he was spending a lot of time with Jordan Chandler but before the allegations occurred. As they spoke at the Los Angeles party of a mutual friend, Presley – then married to another man – asked Michael if he was 'coming on' to her. He said he was. Once Michael was facing the Chandler abuse allegations she and the singer became even closer.

Presley had been addicted to drugs including cocaine in her younger years but was clean by this time. She was therefore able to offer Michael expert support as he battled his own issues with painkillers. She felt she had a duty to save him from ruin. He would need this support. The traumatic experience he was going through as a result of the Chandler case was about to get ever more painful as he was forced to submit to a degrading experience and then watched in horror as one of his own siblings turned on him. On 16 November the police secured a warrant to perform a strip search on Michael. Jordan had given police detailed descriptions of Michael's genital area and of his buttocks. The boy said Michael was circumcised, had pink and brown marks on his scrotum, short pubic hair and blotches on his left buttock. He was out of the country at the time, but as soon as he returned to the United States, Michael would be examined intimately by the authorities. Before this took place there was a slew of developments: Sony Music issued a statement stating its 'unconditional support' of him; MTV Europe follow suit, putting on a 'Michael Jackson Day' on their station; five former Jackson security guards filed lawsuits claiming they were fired because they 'knew too much'; *People* magazine ran the headline 'Michael Jackson Cracks Up – Sex, Drugs and the Fall of the World's Biggest Star'; the *Daily Express* published a story claiming Jermaine was not convinced his brother was innocent (according to Adrian Grant's *Michael Jackson: The Visual Documentary*, Jermaine threatened to sue).

However, in December LaToya truly blew the case open when she gave an extraordinary press conference in Tel Aviv, Israel. 'Michael is my brother and I love him very much,' she began. 'But

I cannot and will not be a silent collaborator in his crimes against young children. If I remain silent, then that means I feel the guilt and humiliation that these children are feeling, and I think it is very wrong. Forget about the superstar, forget about the icon. If he was any other thirty-five-year-old man who was sleeping with little boys, you would not like this guy.' She admitted she had no evidence that Michael had ever harmed a child but carried on nonetheless: 'I am a victim myself [of child abuse]. When parents abuse their children, the children go on to be abusers themselves. Do you know how many children are going to psychiatrists because of Michael? So many, many children.' It was an astonishing statement by LaToya, not least because she admitted that she had not even seen Michael for some years. She was offered – and accepted – a succession of highly lucrative media spots in the weeks that followed her press conference.

The remainder of the Jackson family were quick to refute what LaToya – who had been effectively disowned by the family since she had posed nude for *Playboy* magazine in the late 1980s – had said, including that Katherine had shown her cancelled cheques which had been written to pay off boys who had uncomfortable stories to tell of Michael. 'She's been brainwashed by her money-grabbing mongrel of a husband,' said Katherine of her daughter. When LaToya was told of the family's angry denunciation of her, she stood firm, claiming they were only so supportive of Michael because they depended on his riches for their own livelihoods. Years on, LaToya apologized for all she had said and admitted it had all been made up, under pressure from her husband. However, back in 1993 her words were astonishingly damaging to Michael's

Some of the famous ladies in Michael's life: Liza Minelli in 1983 (*top left*); Elizabeth Taylor in 1992 (*top right*) and Princess Diana in 1988 (*below*).

Michael's early alleged romances: (*above*)
Tatum O'Neal, 1978; (*right*) Stephanie Mills,
1978; (*below*) Brooke Shields, 1984.

Above: Michael and his first wife, Lisa-Marie Presley, whom he married in 1994.

Left: At the 1996 wedding to his second wife, Debbie Rowe.

Michael's natural affinity with both animals and children is well-known. Here he is seen (*top left*) with Corey the Chimp at Universal Studios, Florida, in 1991; at the Heal the World Orphanage in Romania in 1992 (*top right*); and visiting a patient at a children's hospital in Israel, 1993 (*bottom*).

In the nineties, Michael's mesmerising showmanship continued to attract vast audiences for his world tours. Here he is performing in London at his *Dangerous* tour, 1991 (*top left*), and in Prague for the first date of his 1996 *HIStory* tour (*top right*).

In a typically eccentric publicity stunt, Michael promoted his 1995 *HIStory* album by floating a thirty-five-foot statue of himself down the Thames.

Above: Holding a picture of Sony chairman, Tommy Mottola, during his public battle with the record company in July 2002.

Left: A troubled Michael testifies in court during his t for cancelling concert appearances in November t same year.

Left: The notorious 'baby-dangling' incident in Berlin in November 2002.

Below: Entering the courthouse for his trial for child molestation in January 2004. He was later cleared of all charges.

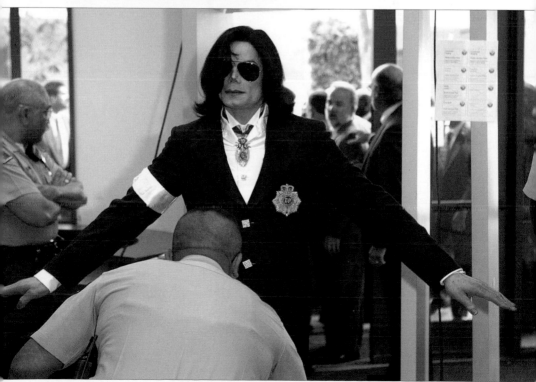

Left: The greatest comeback of all time? Announcing his plans for a summer residency at the O2 Arena in London, March 2009.

Below: The world lost one of its greatest entertainers, but Michael Jackson's children simply lost their dad: Paris, Prince Michael and Prince Michael II at the public memorial concert on 7 July 2009.

KING OF POP
MICHAEL JACKSON
THIS IS IT

embattled reputation. An American radio station removed his music from their play-list. Would others follow suit?

Two days after LaToya's press conference Michael returned to America and prepared to face the humiliation of being strip searched. He had no choice but to go along with the examination. If he refused then that would be admissible evidence in court and would paint him as a man with lots to hide. On 20 December the authorities arrived at Neverland to perform the search. Michael was nervous and sickened by what was ahead. As for the police, they were in electric mood: the following hour could make or destroy the case against Michael. Eventually, after some last-minute delays, Michael stripped in front of the detectives, a doctor, a photographer and the district attorney. 'Oh God,' he sighed as he stared at a picture of Elizabeth Taylor, in a desperate attempt to imagine he was elsewhere. All of the descriptions of his body that Jordan had made were correct, apart from that Michael was not circumcised. However, as it was later pointed out, the foreskin rolls back when a man's penis is erect, which could give the impression of circumcision, particularly to young eyes. Michael terminated the examination at the earliest moment he felt he could and left the room, humiliated. For anyone it would have been upsetting, but for a star used to living life exactly as he wished, it must have been an even tougher experience. 'How could this happen to me?' he asked, puzzled.

Conflicting conclusions were drawn as to whether the examination had or had not damned Michael. It was undeniable that some of Jordan's descriptions had been corroborated by the examination of Michael's genitals. However, supporters of Michael pointed quickly to the swimming pool at Neverland that the singer and Jordan had often swum in together. Might Jordan have seen Michael's genitals while they were changing into swimwear? But then, asked the doubters, how would Jordan have been aware of the markings on the underside of Michael's penis, unless he had (as he claimed) seen it erect? Supporters countered that Jordan's accurate descriptions of the markings on Michael's buttocks could easily have been guessed, given what was publicly known of Michael's skin condition. Round and round the arguments went, never reaching a consensus. Michael insisted to his dying day that the examination had contradicted and not corroborated Jordan's descriptions. He was not alone in his assertion. Reports in 1994 in *USA Today* and Reuters quoted police sources saying that 'photos of Michael Jackson's genitalia do not match' Jordan's descriptions.

Two days later he was to attempt to regain control of public opinion with a four-minute statement delivered to camera. It was originally broadcast on CNN and then picked up by other networks. The world held its breath as it heard the first substantial words delivered direct from Michael on the entire controversy. He was wearing an understated red shirt but his face clearly had a lot of make-up on it. 'I am doing well and I am strong,' he began confidently. 'There have been many disgusting statements made recently concerning allegations of improper conduct on my part. These statements about me are totally false. As I have maintained from the very beginning, I am hoping for a speedy end to this horrifying, horrifying experience to which I have been subjected.' He turned to the media coverage of the case and was scathing. 'I am particularly upset by the handling of this matter by the incredible, terrible mass media…I ask all of you to wait to hear the truth before you label or condemn me.' He called the physical examination 'dehumanising'. He continued: 'It was the most humiliating ordeal of my life – one that no person should ever have to suffer. And even after experiencing the indignity of this search, the parties involved were still not satisfied and wanted to take even more pictures. It was a nightmare, a horrifying nightmare. But if this is what I have to endure to prove my innocence, my complete innocence, so be it.'

It was an effective and convincing performance from Michael. Returning to the allegations themselves, he again refuted them and said: 'If I am guilty of anything, it is of giving all that I have to give to help children all over the world. It is of loving children, of all ages and races, it is of gaining sheer joy from seeing children with their innocent and smiling faces. It is of enjoying, through them, the childhood that I missed myself. If I am guilty of anything, it is of believing what God said about children: "Suffer little children to come unto me and forbid them not, for such is the kingdom of heaven." In no way do I think that I am God, but I do try to be God-like in my heart.' In conclusion he spoke directly to his fans: 'Together we will see this through to the very end. I love you very much and may God bless you all. I love you. Goodbye.' In the wake of the statement many American television shows and newspapers ran polls of their viewers or readers about Michael: all of them found a growing belief in Michael's innocence with 88 per cent of one poll's respondents saying they believed he was not guilty.

His biblical illusion in this statement were repeated in a television interview that he gave in 1996, which only surfaced after his death, in which he spoke about the allegations. 'Jesus said to love the children and be like the children – to be youthful and innocent, and be pure and honourable,' read Michael from a statement he had written earlier. 'He always surrounded himself with children. That's how I was raised – to believe, and to be like that, and to imitate that.' Michael's regular comparisons between himself and Jesus or God might have been well-meant but were ill-advised to say the least, as they did little to dispel public suspicion that he was either mad or deluded or both.

The matter was about to be brought to an end. As the two people at the centre of the story – Michael and Jordan Chandler – continued to suffer emotionally from the pressure of the case, the two parties' legal teams reached an agreement. Michael would pay $22 million to the Chandlers. Evan and June would receive a million each, the rest would go to Jordan in instalments over the coming five years. 'They've worn me down, I admit it,' said Michael, explaining his decision to settle. Presley had been instrumental in his decision, too, telling him that 'a good night's sleep' was more important than the public's opinion of him. It did indeed seem strange to many observers that a man accused of child abuse would settle out of court were he innocent. Surely, people felt, he would want his day in court to formally disprove the allegations? However, the same could be asked in reverse. Why would parents who believed that a man had sexually abused their child accept a payment to not pursue the matter through the normal legal channels? Would their gut instincts not be to want him imprisoned? Surely there could be no 'price' that could be put on such a matter that would make them go away quietly?

Michael strongly believed that his fan base would continue to stand by him and was confident he could pick up his career and move onwards. Only time would tell how much damage the saga had had on his popularity but he was helped by a statement of support from Stevie Wonder, who summed up Michael's experience of late as being akin to a 'witch hunt'. Still, for now he could console himself that the matter was behind him (though Evan Chandler tried unsuccessfully to sue him the following year for breaking the terms of the agreement that prohibited Michael from discussing the case publicly). It had come at a price but he had peace of mind at last. He did not know then that he would face a similar scandal in subsequent years.

Were quieter, less peculiar days ahead for Michael? No, instead he become engaged to and then quickly married the daughter of rock music's biggest ever icon.

CHAPTER FIVE

After being reunited at the Los Angeles home of a mutual friend, Michael and Lisa Marie became closer and closer. The pair stayed in touch and in time their relationship changed from friendship into something more romantic – though as ever nothing was straightforward in Michael-land and an element of ambiguity hung over the relationship. 'We sort of went out together,' Michael later told *Ebony* magazine of how the romance evolved. 'Then we would talk on the phone. I noticed that we had become closer. The brilliant thing about us is that we were often together but did not let anybody know about it. We got to see each other that way over the years. We were really quiet and comfortable with each other. That's pretty much how the dating started happening.'

The public did, in time, get to know about the relationship as the couple became less secretive. They were photographed in June 1994 at Disney World in Florida and also spent time relaxing together at his Neverland ranch. Alongside them were her children Benjamin and Danielle, from her first marriage to musician Danny Keough. If the effect was intended to be that they appeared to the public to be a family unit, it worked. 'It kind of unfolded,' said Michael of how the relationship continued to develop. 'We spent a lot of time on the ranch and we just walked around and talked. It happened! It unfolded all natural. We could just feel the feeling we had for each other, without even talking about it. It was all in the vibrations, the feelings and even the look in our eyes.' Those vibrations and feelings led to Michael spontaneously popping the question. One evening, out of the blue, he proposed to Lisa Marie over the phone. It was a bizarre way to propose marriage and his phrasing of the question was strangely indirect. 'If I asked you to marry me, would you do it?' She replied that she would. Only Michael Jackson could get engaged – by telephone – to the daughter of one of the twentieth century's most famous people.

It was a short engagement and the pair were quickly wed. The story of the marriage was broken on the British breakfast television show *GMTV* on 11 July 1994. It was denied by spokespeople for Michael on CNN, while Presley's spokesperson admitted she could not contact her client. It was not until August that the story was officially confirmed, with Presley releasing a statement and revealing that her married name was Lisa Marie Presley-Jackson. The truth was that they had indeed wed on 26 May 1994, just twenty days after she divorced Keough. The secret, fifteen-minute ceremony took place in La Vega, in the Dominican Republic, and Michael later confessed that he was disappointed that he had not made more of an occasion of it. They said their vows, exchanged gold rings, and that was that – neither invited or even informed their families of the wedding. 'Do you take Lisa Marie to be your wife,' Michael was asked. 'Why not?' he replied. 'It was all very strange,' the judge who wed them told reporters. Michael, inevitably, blamed the media for the fact that they did not have a proper ceremony. The fact that other A-list celebrities enjoyed lavish wedding days did not seem to occur to him, and it was not long until even his new wife was tiring of his victim mentality. In the meantime, some observers speculated that the couple choosing such a curt ceremony was more to do with the guilt they felt over the insincerity of what they were embarking on.

As their families and friends discovered they had wed, many were hurt, including Elizabeth Taylor, who asked friends: 'What has he done?' As for Lisa Marie's mother, Priscilla knew a thing or two about marrying music icons, having wed Elvis Presley at the height of his fame. However, she disapproved of her daughter's relationship with Michael. Priscilla believed that Michael was using her daughter to divert attention from the child abuse allegations and their aftermath. 'It's so obvious,' she told her daughter. Presley's ex-husband Danny Keough also voiced his concerns over his ex-wife's course of action. When reports surfaced that Michael had forced his wife into plastic surgery, her loved ones' fears only grew. Michael denied these stories. He did, however, suggest they hold a séance to discover what his wife's deceased music legend father thought of their union. His wife flatly refused.

She was also bitterly opposed to Michael's last-minute suggestion that they kiss publicly as they opened the eleventh annual MTV Video Awards on 12 September 1994. Minutes before they took to the stage, he told her he was going to kiss her in front of the television cameras. She loudly told him she did not want him to, but once they were on stage he did so regardless: it was the first public kiss the couple enjoyed. 'Just think, nobody said this would last,' Michael joked to the audience. Backstage after their spot his wife was furious with him and much of the media reacted to the kiss with cynicism. Two weeks later he was officially told that no child abuse charges would be brought against him. He said: 'I'm grateful that the investigation has reached its conclusion. I am grateful to my family and friends who have stood by me, and believed in my innocence. Lisa Marie and I look forward to getting on with our lives, raising a family, and will never forget the unending outpouring of love from all over the world. God bless you.' Soon after this, however, the couple were to grant a television interview in which the child abuse saga would be high on the list of questions. Between them they were to do a very bad job of defending Michael on the matter.

The couple were interviewed by Diane Sawyer on ABC's live show *Primetime* on 15 June 1995. It was their first television interview as a couple and Michael's first major interview since his spot on Oprah Winfrey's show two years earlier. It was not to prove a good public relations moment. Sawyer asked Michael what he thought should happen to people who did the sorts of things Chandler had accused him of. Michael replied that they should receive 'help in some kind of way'. Presley-Jackson then said of Michael's ongoing friendships with children: '*They* jump in bed with *him*.' Sawyer asked Presley-Jackson if she would let her son, once he was twelve years of age, sleep with a man in his thirties. Michael's wife stumbled over her answer, saying, 'I know that he's not like that.' When Sawyer asked Michael if he would invite children to share a bed with him in the future, he replied: 'If they want. It's on the level of purity and love and innocence, complete innocence. If you're talking about sex, then that's a nut. It's not me. Go to the guy down the street, 'cause it's not Michael Jackson.'

Presley-Jackson at one point said to Sawyer: 'Do we have sex? Is that what you were going to ask? Yes, YES, Yes!' She denied rumours that their marriage was a publicity stunt, but to an increasing number of observers it seemed just that – a sham. Arguments soon started between the pair, including about Michael's ongoing habit of befriending children. Lisa Marie accused him of being selfish and not considering the implications for her in the public eye. When asked by an Australian magazine if he and his wife were about to split, Michael denied it, saying: 'No, no, no, no'. However, by December 1994 there were already rumours that the couple were to divorce. A public statement was issued via Bob Jones of MJJ Productions: 'It is absolutely unequivocally untrue. Michael Jackson is here in Chicago recording; Ms Jackson is in Los Angeles at her home. They are happy and we are very sad, it is very sad that these people continue to try and make problems.' Some thirteen months later the marriage would indeed be over. First, though, Michael had an album to release and promote.

* * *

The original tracks for the new album were recorded in New York during the winter of 1994/95. Among them were some of his most memorable recordings, including the R. Kelly-penned 'You Are Not Alone', 'Earth Song' (which he wrote in an Austrian hotel room) and 'Scream', the latter written with the help of sister

Janet who dueted with him on the recording. Memorable for the wrong reasons was the song 'They Don't Care About Us', which was a tirade against those who he felt were against him. It included the lines 'Jew me, sue me, everybody do me' and 'Kike me, don't you black or white me'. These lyrics were naturally interpreted as anti-Semitic, a charge he denied. 'The idea that these lyrics could be deemed objectionable is extremely hurtful to me, and mislead-ing,' he said in a statement. 'I very much regret and apologize from the bottom of my heart if I have hurt anyone's feelings.' He re-recorded the vocals as a result of the controversy, but this was too late to prevent the song being pulled from the playlists of MTV and VH1 in April 1996. (He was accused of being prejudiced against Jewish people again in 2005 when the ABC television show *Good Morning America* broadcast a recording of him speaking to an adviser about Jewish people: 'They suck… they're like leeches. It's a conspiracy. The Jews do it on purpose.' He denied being anti-Semitic, telling *Entertainment Tonight*: 'By the way, I love Jewish people.') The original songs formed the second disc in a double-CD album, the first disc of which was a greatest hits affair including tracks such as 'Billie Jean' and 'Thriller'. In full the album's title was *HIStory: Past, Present and Future, Book 1*.

To promote the album Michael had quite a trick up his sleeve. He commissioned a thirty-five-foot fibreglass statue to be made of him. It was floated down the River Thames in London during the week of the album's release. The same stunt was pulled in other European capital cities. It was an eye-catching and memorable public relations trick but rather confirmed in the eyes of many that

Michael's ego was out of control and that he had lost any semblance of normality or self-awareness in his life. He also captured the headlines with the Wayne Isham-directed video for 'You Are Not Alone', as it showed him and his wife playing around half naked. Given the intense public interest in their relationship and the secretive way they conducted much of their business, this was a surprise move which had tongues wagging and helped make the single the first ever song to go straight to number one in America. The album sold 15 million copies around the world – Michael's sales were in decline, returning to the level of *Off the Wall*. He and his record company were stung by talk that the album was a flop and took out a two-page advertisement in *Billboard* magazine boasting of its commercial successes.

In September 1995, Michael gave another landmark performance of his career. At the twelfth annual MTV Music Video Awards he performed a medley of his songs: 'Don't Stop 'Til You Get Enough'/'The Way You Make Me Feel'/'Scream'/'Beat It'/'Black or White'/'Billie Jean'/'Dangerous'/'Smooth Criminal'/'You Are Not Alone'. He took to the stage during the spoken introduction to 'Don't Stop 'Til You Get Enough' but killed the song dead at the point at which it normally kicks into life. He then stared defiant and motionless into the audience, who had been whipped into quite a frenzy by the drama. Finally, the music returned and he bopped to 'The Way You Make Me Feel'. By now he had removed his jacket and the music segued into 'Scream'. He nodded proudly as it quickly spun into 'Beat It' and then 'Black or White', for which he was joined onstage by the rock guitarist Slash. Michael stood in a jet of smoke at the front of the stage, arms out wide, in full Messianic mode, as Slash brought the guitar track to a finale. The singer even managed some headbanging as a literal nod to the rock sound booming through the theatre.

Oh, the showmanship. Michael ran around the stage 'throwing fire' by timing his arm movements perfectly to the onstage pyrotechnics. He was incorrigible. Slash, who seemed to be outstaying his welcome, was motioned to leave the stage by both a member of the stage crew and Michael himself but was still playing guitar when the familiar, iconic drum track introduction to 'Billie Jean' rocked the venue. Michael had donned a spangly black jacket and a hat and a huge silhouette of him covered the white curtain at the back of the stage. He then appeared onstage with the hat removed. Then the hat was back and he grabbed his groin and thrusted as he danced on: Moonwalking, strutting and delighting the audience. Again, at the song's conclusion, came the Messianic pose: arms outstretched, head tipped back and eyes closed as the audience bombarded him with astonished love. The traumas he had been through in the Jordan Chandler affair must have seemed a distant memory to him. The audience, on its feet, must have momentarily forgotten them. 'Thank you,' he said, his voice humble in comparison to his body language just moments before. 'Slash, you're amazing! For those who like living danger-ously,' he continued, 'this one's for you.' As 'Dangerous' kicked in, a troupe of Michael lookalikes, dressed identically to him, abseiled onto the stage. Each one was then 'shot' leaving just Michael standing, before they joined him in an intricately choreographed dance. The evening had seen nothing to compare with this, neither had – arguably – pop history. There was even time for a blast of

'Smooth Criminal' and 'You Are Not Alone' before he accepted his final, hysterical acclaim from the crowd. His stint had not merely upstaged the rest of the performers that evening, it had stunned all who witnessed it. The other acts at the show dropped their cool exteriors to praise Michael, and scrambled to get a view of his performance from the wings. Michael had been simply, imperiously, wonderful.

Proving less successful was his marriage to Lisa Marie, their troubles underscored when Michael took a holiday in Paris with two friends but without his wife. By this time, a new woman had entered his imagination. He had first met Debbie Rowe – the adopted daughter of a millionaire Malibu couple – in the 1980s when she worked as a receptionist for Michael's dermatologist Dr Arnold Klein. As his marriage with Presley-Jackson collapsed, his friendship with Rowe intensified. They were obsessed with one another and were soon speaking on the telephone several times a day. Presley-Jackson took to referring to Rowe as 'Nursey'. Michael's wife was proving unwilling to mother children for him, fearing the legal complications such a move would bring in the event of an increasingly likely divorce. Michael challenged his wife that if she would not do it then Rowe was willing to mother children for him. Lisa Marie called his bluff and told him to go ahead with that route to fatherhood.

Which he did. Rowe was soon pregnant, though mystery surrounds whether Michael was the father or not and whether she was impregnated naturally or via artificial insemination. She miscarried this child but was soon pregnant again. By this time, Michael and Lisa Marie Presley-Jackson had divorced. The divorce was announced on 18 January 1996 on CNN and reported the following day in *USA Today*. Presley-Jackson had filed for the divorce with the date of separation cited by her as 10 December 1995. Michael's spokesman confirmed the report, saying that the couple had 'mutually agreed to go their separate ways. However, they remain good friends.' The divorce was finalized in August 1996, with his ex-wife receiving 10 per cent of the royalties of the *HIStory* album as part of her settlement. It had been a short marriage, but in truth few were surprised when it ended so quickly. Lisa Marie denied she had married Michael to further her own musical career ambitions, telling Diane Sawyer in a subsequent television interview: 'I'm not gonna marry someone for a recording career.'

Between the announcement and the finalizing of the divorce, Michael had hit the headlines for a different reason. He gave his first live television performance in England for two decades at the Brit Awards on 19 February 1996. There he would sing the *HIStory* track 'Earth Song', accompanied by over sixty children. It was another somewhat Messianic-styled performance from Michael: he was dressed in a white robe and surrounded by children. During the performance he was lifted from the stage and it was then that controversy struck. Jarvis Cocker was at this point a Britpop icon thanks to being lead vocalist in the successful indie band Pulp. Watching Michael's performance, Cocker – who admitted he had sunk a few drinks that evening – became sickened by the entire spectacle. He spontaneously decided to mount his own protest. He did this by taking to the stage and wiggling his backside at Michael. He was grabbed by security officers, led from the stage and arrested.

'My actions were a form of protest at the way Michael Jackson sees himself as some kind of Christ-like figure with the power of healing,' Cocker said later. 'The music industry allows him to indulge his fantasies because of his wealth and power. People go along with it even though they know it's a bit sick. I just couldn't go along with it any more. It was a spur-of-the-moment decision brought on by boredom and frustration.' To some, Cocker's actions made him a hero but others suspected his 'frustration' was born out of Michael's fame, and it was pointed out that three children were hurt in the scuffle that broke out during his removal from the stage. Fellow Britpop star Damon Albarn of Blur has since criticized Cocker's actions, saying: 'I found it really disturbing when he pulled his pants down in front of Michael Jackson – that just seemed really wrong.' After Michael's death, Cocker spoke again about the episode. 'Rock stars have big enough egos without pretending to be Jesus,' he said on BBC1's *Question Time* show, 'that was what got my goat, that one particular thing.'

Later in the evening at the Brits Michael had the last laugh when he accepted the Artist of a Generation award. 'I am humbled by this award,' he said, 'especially coming from my wonderful family in the United Kingdom. You have provided me with so much love and support in my career.' Only on the following day did he refer to Cocker's protest, in a statement issued by his record company. 'Michael Jackson respects Pulp as artists but is totally shocked by their behaviour and utterly fails to understand their complete lack of respect for fellow artists and performers. His main concern is for people that worked for him and the fact that children should be attacked. He feels sickened, saddened, shocked, upset, cheated, angry but is immensely proud that the cast remained professional and the show went on.'

* * *

In November, while Michael was busy on a world tour to promote *HIStory*, it was revealed in the *San Francisco Chronicle* that Debbie Rowe was pregnant with Michael's 'first child'. The British tabloid the *News of the World* followed up on the story later that month, under the headline 'I am having Jacko's baby'. The lurid article claimed that she would receive half a million pounds for carrying Michael's baby, which it said had been conceived via artificial insemination. It was also noted that, given the timing of the pregnancy, she must have conceived while Michael had still been married to Presley-Jackson. Rowe was furious, feeling that she and Michael were being treated like 'freaks'. Welcome to his world, Debbie. In the wake of this report Rowe's father spoke to the media of his 'shock' when his daughter had dropped the bombshell that she was carrying Michael's child. Michael's mother Katherine was upset to learn her son had fathered a child out of wedlock and publicly compared his actions with those of his father in the 1970s – a comparison that must have hurt Michael deeply.

Katherine also spoke with Rowe and gave her a lengthy lecture about how important love, loyalty and marriage were to her. With Michael already feeling immense guilt and upset over the comparison his mother had drawn between himself and his father, there was plenty of pressure on him to 'do the decent thing'. The upshot was that within a week of this discussion, Michael and Debbie

Rowe were married. The civil ceremony took place on 15 November 1996 and took the world by surprise. It was not exactly expected by Rowe, either. Michael had summoned her to Australia, where he and his entourage were staying at the Sheraton on the Park hotel in Sydney. She had no idea that he planned to ask her to marry him once she arrived, jetlagged from the long flight.

Only a handful of friends and tour staff attended the ceremony in the Presidential Suite. The bride and groom both wore black, and Michael's best man was an eight-year-old boy called Anthony who he had recently befriended. It did not escape the attention of many that the boy was very similar in appearance to Jordan Chandler. In the wake of the ceremony, Michael issued a short statement. 'Please respect our privacy and let us enjoy this wonderful and exciting time,' it read. This was hardly the most romantic of statements and did not hint at any considerable wedded bliss. As for Rowe, her words were hardly brimful of wonderment in the wake of the ceremony. She telephoned a friend and when asked whether she loved her husband replied: 'Yes I do, sort of.' She told another friend that she and Michael had slept in separate rooms on their wedding night. The following evening Michael went to a film premiere. At his side was not his wife, but his eight-year-old friend Anthony. The *Daily Mirror* photographed Rowe with her head in her hands on her hotel balcony. The headline read: 'Oh my God! I've just married Michael Jackson!'

The following year, in February 1997, Rowe gave birth to Michael's son at Cedars-Sinai Medical Center in Los Angeles, where Michael had been taken after his accident filming the Pepsi commercial the previous decade. Michael was present at the birth and helped his wife cut the umbilical cord. 'Words can't describe how I feel,' said Michael in a statement. 'I have been blessed beyond comprehension and I will work tirelessly at being the best father I can possibly be. I appreciate that my fans are elated but I hope that everyone respects the privacy that Debbie and I want and need for our son. I grew up in a fishbowl and will not allow that to happen to my child. Please respect our wishes and give my son his privacy.' The baby was called Prince Michael I and was quickly whisked away to Neverland by Michael. Rowe was not to see her baby again for six weeks, when she was called to the Four Seasons hotel to pose for a photo shoot for *OK!* magazine. Indeed, in the coming months mother and child would rarely see each other. Instead, a team of nurses and nannies raised Prince Michael I at Neverland, under constant video surveillance. Hygiene was also regularly monitored: the quality of air in his room was measured on the hour and toys were replaced with fresh versions daily. Interviewed on ABC's *20/20* television show, Michael said that when his son cried, he would dance in front of him to stop the tears.

* * *

As one significant life began, another ended. In the early hours of 31 August 1997, Diana, Princess of Wales, was killed in a car accident in Paris. Michael had become friendly with Diana after meeting her at Wembley and felt he could identify with the way she became an obsession for the world's media. When news reached him of her death he was devastated and cancelled the following day's concert in Ostend, Belgium. He then issued a statement that read: 'The sudden loss of Diana, Princess of Wales, is one of the greatest tragedies of the millennium. She was a friend to the world. As one who has been under scrutiny the majority of my life, I speak with authority when I say that I am horrified that the paparazzi, supported by the tabloids' animalistic behaviour, may be acceptable to the public. It is totally unwarranted in a civilized society. The world's acceptance of the practise if continued will accelerate tragedies of this magnitude.' He later attended a memorial service for Diana at St James's Episcopal Church in Los Angeles. Her death had prompted extraordinary, perhaps unprecedented scenes of public mourning across the world and the story become a media obsession for weeks. The like of which was not seen again until Michael himself died twelve years later.

The same year, Michael released *Blood on the Dance Floor: HIStory in the Mix.* The thirteen-track album comprised eight remixes from the *HIStory* album and five brand new tracks including the title song, which was the updated take on a tune originally intended for inclusion on *Dangerous.* Another original was 'Morphine', a song about drug abuse which included an audio clip from Michael's beloved song 'The Elephant Man'. The album was dedicated to Elton John, who had supported the singer during his woes of 1993. The album did not fare well, selling around 7 million copies worldwide and doing badly in America. The *New York Daily News* was scathing in its reception, saying the album's lyrics were ruined by. 'Predatory women, jealous underlings and the evil media...He's once again playing victim – the world's most powerless billionaire, it seems – mewling about forces conspiring against his heavenly self.' The album's disappointing sales were noted in the industry and while Michael remained a media obsession, his stature in the eyes of many in music business circles was already on the decline. All the same, he could point to the success of the *HIStory* world tour that year which netted $83,513,126. This was hardly the stuff of disaster.

A year after their surprise marriage, Debbie and Michael announced that she was pregnant with their second child. The couple said the child had been conceived in Paris, so they planned to call their daughter Paris Michael Katherine Jackson. Rowe, who described the child as a 'gift' for Michael, gave birth at 6.26 a.m. on 3 April 1998. However, the 'gift' was not enough to save the marriage which had obviously been in jeopardy for some time. Michael had been seeing more of his ex-wife Lisa Marie Presley and was spending more time with new young male friends than he was with Rowe, who refused to tell reporters whether the couple ever had sex. 'What happens behind closed doors is our business,' she said. The couple agreed to divorce in October 1999. 'Michael and Debbie remain friends and they ask that the public respect their desire not to further comment or speculate upon the reasons for their decision,' read a statement issued via a spokesman. Sources claim that Michael gave his ex-wife $10 million in settlement. It was not the last the public would hear of the matter and in the wake of his death, Michael's relationship with Rowe and the parenthood of his children would become the matter of intensive scrutiny and debate.

Meanwhile, he had been inducted into the Rock and Roll Hall of Fame in March 2001, the youngest ever inductee in history. He had achieved so much for a man his age and had begun work on his next album, which would be the first entirely original album he had released in ten years. Some said it was the most expensive album Sony ever issued, with figures as high as $40 million quoted in production fees, though insiders say that he was at best half-hearted in his work on the songs. *Invincible* was released in October 2001 and as a promotional gimmick it was available in four different colours: blue, green, red and gold. Among the stand-out songs was 'You Rock My World' which he co-wrote with Rodney Jerkins, who was a long-term fan of Michael. Another was 'Butterflies' which he co-wrote with Brit Marsha Ambrosius. She recalled how he would consult with her during the recording, despite his vastly superior experience and stature. The only track he wrote alone was 'Speechless', which had a typically eccentric genesis. 'I was with these kids in Germany,' Michael revealed during a web chat, 'and we had a big water balloon fight. I was so happy after the fight that I ran upstairs in the house and I wrote "Speechless". Fun inspires me. Out of the bliss comes magic, wonderment and creativity.'

The album sold disappointingly, though, and received scathing reviews from many critics. Alex Petridis wrote in the *Guardian*: 'The songs are unmemorable, not a "Scream" or "Billie Jean" among them. After seventy-six unremitting minutes, you're left in no doubt: like its creator, *Invincible* has simply gone too far.' The *New York Times* complained that: 'There's no joy or humour in it, no sense of release...Pop is a promise of pleasure, but on *Invincible*, he's so busy trying to dazzle listeners that he forgets to have any fun.' *Entertainment Weekly* was damning too, and concluded that Michael was 'Pop's lost boy'. The *NME* was more favourable, concluding that '*Invincible* is a relevant and rejuvenated comeback album made overlong.' *Rolling Stone* magazine said that *Invincible* places the listener 'squarely in Michael Jacksonland…It's an excruciatingly self-referential place, worsened further by its namesake's unmatched controversies and weirdnesses, plus the inevitable march of pop time.' The album ultimately shifted 8 million copies worldwide.

This figure puts the budget into perspective: around this time Justin Timberlake sold the same number of his album *Justified*, which had cost one fifth of what *Invincible* had. Michael was soon in dispute with Sony, over a number of issues regarding the rights to the masters of his back catalogue. The artist and his label were quickly at loggerheads after Sony refused to release his song 'What More Can I Give' in the wake of the 9/11 attacks on America. Michael then held a press conference accusing the head of the label, Tommy Mottola, of being racially prejudiced. 'He's mean, he's a racist, and he's very, very, very devilish,' stormed Michael. He then named a black artist, and said that Mottola had 'called him a fat black nigger…And I can't deal with that, you know. It's wrong.' He added the accusation that the label failed to promote *Invincible* properly. Sony disputed all his claims, which they called 'spiteful and hurtful'. In a public statement, Sony said: 'It seems particularly bizarre that he has chosen to launch an unwarranted and ugly attack on an executive [Mottola] who has championed his career.' Sony said that it was 'appalled that Mr Jackson would stoop so low in his constant quest for publicity'.

* * *

In 2002, Michael's third child was born by an unnamed mother who Michael said he never met. The boy was named Prince Michael II, but was given the nickname 'Blanket' by Michael and those close to him. The word 'blanket' had become a term that Michael said meant, effectively, 'blessing'. There has naturally been much speculation over the identity of the woman who birthed Blanket. Since Michael's death there have even been assertions that he is not the father of Blanket or the other two children. There is no sign of resolution on these questions, but it is fair to say that Michael's arrangements for parenthood were as unconventional as one can imagine.

Ironically, the child was under a blanket when he made his first major – and highly controversial – public appearance. Michael arrived in Berlin on 19 November 2002, with his three children in tow. Staying in the lush Presidential Suite of the Aldon Hotel, opposite the Brandenburg Gate, he became aware of the customary hordes of fans outside. He went onto his balcony and waved to them. Then, he had an idea…

Some of the fans were shouting about Michael's children, particularly his recently born son, who they asked to see. Despite being four floors up and fifty feet above the pavement, Michael dangled his son over the edge of his balcony. He was holding the baby, covered in a blanket, with one arm around his waist. It was hardly a safe manoeuvre; nevertheless the fans cheered and within seconds Michael was back in his room. That might have been the end of it, but some of the fans had videoed the incident and the footage soon found its way to television networks around the world. It was a relatively slow news day and the media leapt on the story, repeating the footage over and over on rolling news channels. This scene of irresponsibility from Michael became the talk of the globe. The following morning the newspapers were awash with stories of outrage. The *Sun* headlined its front page story 'You Lunatic' and the *Daily Mirror* dubbed him a 'Mad Bad Dad' and called for the Berlin police to arrest the singer. Child protection groups around the world also criticized Michael. As for the fans, they continued to support him, chanting: 'Fuck the press, you're the best' from outside the hotel.

This was a public relations disaster for Michael. He had worked to try to shed much of his 'Wacko Jacko' image and had also tried to counter the suspicions that he had abused children. Yet here he was dangling his blanket-covered son over the railings of a fourth-floor hotel balcony. 'Every time you think you've got to the bottom of his weirdness, this guy just keeps topping himself,' a contributing editor to *Rolling Stone* magazine said. 'I completely fear for his children. Child welfare should just go in there now with a regime change.' Michael was forced to apologize as the story began to spin out of control. 'I offer no excuses for what happened,' he said. 'I made a terrible mistake. I got caught up in the excitement of the moment. I would never intentionally endanger the lives of my children.' The Berlin blanket episode became one of the most defining images of the latter stages of Michael's life. The following summer rap artist Eminem paid a sarcastic tribute to the episode when he appeared at the window of his Scotland hotel wearing a black and white tracksuit and surgical mask and dangled a blanket-covered baby doll in the air to the amusement of onlookers.

Michael would not have found Eminem's stunt funny as he

counted the cost of a public relations disaster. How could a man with four decades of experience in the limelight have made such an unwise – and potentially tragic – error in front of the world?

However, he was about to make a far, far worse mistake...

CHAPTER SIX

In retrospect, Michael Jackson should have seen Martin Bashir coming a mile off. When the British broadcasting journalist approached him to make a television show for ITV, he explained that he wanted unlimited access to Michael's private life for several months, with television cameras following his every move. He also demanded that during his interviews with the star, no subject would be off-limits. This was clearly going to be no fawning process to produce an anodyne outcome. Bashir spent almost five years convincing Michael to co-operate with him. He finally he got the answer he wanted in 2002 and production swiftly began on the programme that was to become *Living with Michael Jackson*. Bashir and his cameras were to be at Michael's side regularly for eight months. The resulting documentary was sensational and – for Michael – upsetting and shocking.

Living with Michael Jackson aired on 3 February 2003 on Britain's ITV channel. It had been heavily hyped ahead of transmission and 15 million people sat down to watch the ninety-minute show, more than had watched the Queen's Jubilee concert. They were amazed at what they saw. Bashir followed Michael across

America and beyond, watching Michael at work, at leisure, shopping and being a parent. At one point, while shopping in Las Vegas, Michael spent millions of dollars in a matter of minutes. Meanwhile, footage of him as a father was scarcely less eye-opening. He sat with Prince Michael II on his knee. The child had his face covered with a scarf and Michael manically bounced the baby on his knee as he fed him milk. The singer even pulled off a – very convincing – impersonation of a cockney accent at one point. The pop icon who had for so long been a mysterious figure had truly opened his life to the world.

But was that a good idea? Revealing as all this footage was, it was Michael's interviews with Bashir that formed the most sensational aspects of the programme. As promised, Bashir quizzed him on all aspects of his tumultuous life and Michael rarely came out of these encounters well. For instance, when Bashir asked him about plastic surgery, Michael flatly denied having undergone any such treatment. 'I've had no plastic surgery on my face, just my nose,' he said, to the obvious disbelief of his interlocutor. 'It helped me breathe better, so I can hit the higher notes. I'm telling you the honest truth. I don't do anything to my face.' Bashir was unconvinced, as would be the viewers at home. The closest Michael came to coming clean during the interview was when he snapped: 'Everybody in Hollywood gets plastic surgery. Plastic surgery was not invented for Michael Jackson.' Denying a fact as obvious as his plastic surgery meant that when Michael denied other – more grave – things in the future, fewer people believed him.

Inevitably, much of the talk centred on Michael's relationship with children. Again, he shot himself in the foot with nearly everything he said. Recalling the birth of his daughter should have been a relatively safe area. Here he could portray himself as a loving father, no different to any other dad. Instead, he said of the birth: 'I was so anxious to get her home after cutting the cord – I hate to say this – I snatched her and just went home with the placenta and everything all over her. I just got her in a towel and ran.' Bashir asked him about the incident in Berlin, when he had perilously dangled his second son over the edge of a hotel balcony. Far from seeming contrite, Michael seemed at best defensive and at worst deluded when he seemingly batted away the concerns over the incident. 'We were waving to thousands of fans below and they were chanting to see my child,' he said turning between Bashir and the camera, 'and I was kind enough to let them see.'

Michael spoke at length about his love of children. As ever, his words could be interpreted in many ways. 'I'll say it a million times. I'm not afraid to say it: if there were no children on this earth, if somebody announced that all kids are dead, I would jump off the balcony immediately,' he said. Were these the words of a loving, caring man or those of a crackpot? Viewers were divided. The most disturbing footage was in the scenes where Michael was interviewed alongside twelve-year-old cancer patient Gavin Arvizo. He held hands with his young friend during the segment and admitted he had slept in the same room as the boy. Arvizo had first met Michael in 2002 after the cancer-battling boy's wish to meet his hero was granted. He and his parents and siblings had stayed with Michael at Neverland and travelled with the singer. It was like the relationship with the Chandler family all over again. Arvizo's mother Janet allegedly encouraged her children to call Michael 'Daddy'. However, much of what occurred during these days and nights was to become highly contentious in due course.

On camera, Bashir asked Gavin what made Michael connect so well with children. 'Because he's really a child at heart,' answered the boy, later saying of Michael: 'He's four,' to the agreement of the singer. Gavin then agreed he had slept in the same room as Michael. After the Chandler case had threatened his career, it was surprising to many viewers that Michael still shared his bedroom with children. Michael was unapologetic. 'I feel sorry for them,' he said of people who thought his behaviour strange, adding that people who would question the arrangement were 'ignorant'. Under questioning from Bashir, Michael remained unrepentant about his relationship with boys. 'I have slept in a bed with many children,' he told the interviewer. 'Why can't you share your bed? That's the most loving thing to do, to share your bed with someone. When you say "bed", you're thinking sexual. They make that sexual; it's not sexual. We're going to sleep, I tuck them in and I put a little music on, and when it's story time, I read a book. We go to sleep with the fireplace on. I give them hot milk, you know, we have cookies. It's very charming, it's very sweet; it's what the whole world should do.' Given that Michael had a family of his own by this time, it seemed even more perturbing that he would have relationships such as these with other people's children. Far from lifting suspicion, his becoming a parent only heightened the oddity of him sleeping in the same room as other people's children particularly as they always seemed to be male. He was uncompromising in the face of Bashir's questions, however. 'My greatest inspiration comes from kids,' he told him. 'It's all inspired from that level of innocence. I just love being around that all the time.'

Michael had not expected the final cut of the programme to be as damning as it was. He was horrified by the edit, feeling Bashir had abused his trust. He quickly issued a public statement. 'I trusted Martin Bashir to come into my life and that of my family because I wanted the truth to be told,' it began. 'Martin Bashir persuaded me to trust him that this would be an honest and fair portrayal of my life and told me that he was "the man that turned Diana's life around". I am heartbroken that someone whom I treated as a friend could stoop so low. Today I feel more betrayed than ever before; that someone who had got to know my children, my staff and me, whom I let into my heart and told the truth, could then sacrifice the trust I placed in him and produce this terrible and unfair programme. It breaks my heart that anyone could truly believe that I would do anything to harm or endanger my children: they are the most important things in my life. Everyone who knows me will know the truth which is that my children come first in my life and that I would never harm any child.'

He further claimed that footage of his children had been included 'contrary to my express consent' and also said he had not been given the chance to view the documentary prior to its broadcast, despite promises this would be permitted. The truth was that he *was* shown the documentary ahead of transmission date, albeit not long before. He was stunned by the programme and knew – say associates – within minutes that the programme was not to be the glowing character reference that he had hoped for:

quite the contrary, in fact. The press and public became more convinced than ever that he was untrustworthy in the wake of the programme, which was shown on American television seventy-two hours after its British premiere. Thirty-eight million Americans tuned in to watch it and viewers Stateside were just as aghast as those in Britain. Michael had another major public relations disaster to try to turn round. He was not the only person to be horrified by the programme, so too were numerous psychologists and child-protection workers who spoke out in fierce condemnation of the singer's behaviour.

Three days later the rearguard action continued when his ex-wife Debbie Rowe was wheeled out to appear on British breakfast television show *GMTV*. 'He is a wonderful, caring man and he's not portrayed as he really is,' she insisted. 'There could be no other person that could be a better father and I resent anyone making allegations that he is not a proper parent. No one has ever read more about parenting, no one has ever practised the art of parenting more, and parenting is an art, you earn the title parent. I believe that there are some people who should be parents and he's one of them, and he is such a fabulous man and such a good friend and he's always been there for me, always, from the day I met him.' Her defence seemed over-zealous to many viewers, who remained unconvinced that the man they had seen manically bouncing his child on his knee during the show, and dangling him over a hotel balcony months earlier, was as perfect a parent as his ex-wife insisted.

The next move from the Jackson camp had a more convincing effect. Bashir had been damning of Michael's parenting skills during his voiceover on the broadcast of *Living with Michael Jackson*. 'The children are restricted,' he concluded, 'I came away quite saddened and deeply disturbed by what I saw.' Yet Michael had in his possession unbroadcast footage of Bashir praising his parenting skills. 'Your relationship with your kids is fantastic,' Bashir is seen telling him. 'In fact, it almost makes me weep when I see you with them because your interaction is so natural, so loving and so caring. Everyone that comes into contact with you knows that.' While interviewers often ingratiate themselves with the celebrities they are working with, this footage – when set against Bashir's subsequent conclusions – did paint him in a disingenuous light. Michael commissioned a counter-documentary that included this footage and fresh interviews with his family, friends and staff in which they insisted that he would never harm children.

It was an effective ploy. The show was originally broadcast on Fox in America and then, four days later, on Sky One in Britain. After the Sky One broadcast, viewers were polled as to whether they thought Bashir had treated Michael unfairly: 92 per cent responded that they thought he had. Soon, news reports began to be printed questioning Bashir's character. 'He was the swerviest man on earth,' one former colleague was quoted as saying in the *Independent*. 'He is incredibly charming, but such a slippery character.' All the same, these reports were drops in an ocean of bad press that Michael faced in the wake of the programme. He felt that Bashir had tried to 'kill' his career and in subsequent years many would come to the conclusion that that was exactly what *Living with Michael Jackson* had done. It was repeated after Michael's death, with the Arvizo footage removed.

Not that the documentary had only unhappy legacies. The most positive result of its broadcast was a thawing of relations between Michael and his father. Michael spoke movingly on the programme of the brutality he had faced from his father as a child. 'He had this belt in his hand,' he said, remembering Jackson 5 rehearsals. 'If you didn't do it in the right way, he would tear you up, really get you. It was bad. Real bad.' Having watched his son's harrowing descriptions, Joseph contacted Michael and – together with Katherine – spent some days at Neverland. There, father and son spent several afternoons talking things over and attempting to put their differences behind them. There were some tense, angry moments but by the time his parents left several days later, Michael was more at peace with his father than he had ever been. This was a significant and welcome development in Michael's life, but scant consolation when compared to what happened in the programme's wake – his arrest on fresh charges of child abuse.

On 18 November 2003, nine months after *Living with Michael Jackson* was broadcast, Michael was staying at the Mirage Hotel in Las Vegas. Meanwhile, back at his Neverland ranch, seventy police officers were raiding his home. Fourteen hours later they left, armed with evidence. Two days later he flew back by private jet to California to face the music. He presented himself at Santa Barbara County jail where he was charged with nine counts of 'lewd and lascivious acts' against his young *Living with...* co-star Gavin Arvizo. Seven of these related to child molestation and the other two were of administering an intoxicating agent for the purpose of committing a felony. Full details would emerge in court. The charging process was a humiliating experience for him.

He was fingerprinted, photographed and forced to surrender his passport. He was freed on bail of $3 million. 'Michael is unequivocally and absolutely innocent of these charges,' his lawyer Mark Geragos told the media, who snapped up the mug shot of Michael that had been taken by the authorities. 'These characters always seem to surface with dreadful allegations just as another project, an album, a video is being released,' said a statement from the Jackson camp. It also damned what it described as 'hucksters and self-styled "inside sources"…guessing and fabricating information about an investigation they couldn't possibly know about'. A friend told the press that they were worried Michael would commit suicide in the face of a fresh set of allegations. No wonder – if found guilty of the charges he knew he could face around twenty years in prison.

At the end of the year, he gave an interview to CBS's *60 Minutes* show. He once more denied the allegations, saying they were: 'Totally false. Before I would hurt a child, I would slit my wrists. I would never hurt a child. It's totally false. I was outraged. I would never do something like that.' Again, an attempt to use television to counter unfortunate headlines had been far from perfect in its execution. The talk of suicide in the same breath as talk of child abuse just lent more weight to the allegations in the eyes of some viewers. His claim that he had been assaulted during his charging in November was also ill-judged. With no evidence to support his claim, and plentiful video evidence to disprove it, it backfired. All the same, his family added weight to his denial, saying in a joint statement: 'We proudly stand next to Michael who we know could never commit any of the acts he is accused of. We will fight with every ounce of our energy to reveal the truth behind these false allegations and the motivations behind those who have falsely accused Michael.' On 20 December six hundred family members and friends of Michael gathered at Neverland for a show of solidarity with the singer, dubbing the event You Are Not Alone.

The Arvizo family had – prior to making the accusations against Michael – denied on numerous occasions that anything untoward had happened between the singer and their son. This included during interviews with social workers from the Los Angeles Department of Child and Family Services. Gavin told the social workers that 'Michael is like a father to me' and added that 'he has never done anything to me sexually'. His mother Janet reiterated this message, saying: 'Michael is like a father to my children. He loves them and I trust my children with him.' Similarly, Gavin's father David said there was 'no reason' to believe Michael had harmed his son. What, wondered Michael's supporters, happened for the Arvizos to subsequently change their story and insist that Michael had mistreated their son? This wasn't the first time the Arvizo family had started litigation. In August 1998 the family settled out of court with the JC Penney department store after Janet claimed that security guards had assaulted her and her sons when Gavin was accused of leaving the shop without paying for the clothes he was carrying. Significantly, only after two years had passed from the alleged assault did Janet add the claim that she had been 'sexually fondled' by the guards. Tom Griffin, who represented JC Penney in that case, described the Arvizos as pursuing a 'scam'.

The allegations made by the family against Michael were being considered in a similar light by those closest to him, but the singer would have to face them in court. His initial hearing was on 16 January 2004 at the Santa Maria court. He arrived late, flanked by bodyguards and relatives and the judge ticked him off for his tardiness. Hundreds of fans had assembled outside the court and as he left he treated them to an impromptu show, jumping onto the roof of the car and dancing before blowing them kisses and flashing a 'V for victory' sign. Invitations were then handed out to fans by Michael's team, inviting them for refreshments at the Neverland ranch. The following day he released a statement of thanks to his fans for supporting him. He knew the value of keeping on good terms with his fans not just for his career, but for his chances of winning the impending trial. Were his fan base to desert him the chances of a jury being sympathetic to his cause were surely reduced. In March he launched a website to communicate with fans, thus avoiding the words of unappointed 'spokespeople' gaining undue credence.

Between then and the beginning of the case proper in January 2005, Michael continued to live life as normally as he could – well, normal by his standards in any case. He travelled to Washington to lobby legislators to spend more resources on battling Aids in Africa and was presented with an award for this work at the city's Ethiopian Embassy. He celebrated his forty-sixth birthday in August and held a party for over two hundred disadvantaged children at Neverland in December. All the while, however, the Arvizo case was an unwelcome presence in his life. It was unavoidable. Indeed, he attended some of the preliminary hearings, wearing white to symbolize innocence. The court received a death threat against Michael via the internet.

The twenty-six-year-old Canadian responsible was traced and given a year's probation.

Finally, on 31 January 2005, the court case began, presided over by the officious but occasionally humorous Judge Rodney Melville. It was, in the eyes of many, 'the trial of the century'. That it was to be a huge event for the media had never been in doubt. However, the vista that greeted those arriving on the first day was like something out of a Tom Wolfe novel. A 480-square-foot stage had been erected outside the court for reporters from *just one network* to use for its coverage. Beyond it there were areas for reporters from other networks and newspapers from across the world to use, including CNN who also had their own stage from which to report on the drama. Others made do with tents or rented space in buildings overlooking the court. There were legions of hair and make-up teams, ready to spruce up the reporters before they went on-air to convey the latest development, however minor. Coffee Diem – a café near the courthouse – did astonishingly high trade every day as the media, fans and other onlookers queued up to buy coffee and snacks. By the end of the trial the café's proprietor was reported to be buying a brand new BMW with the profits. There were even bomb squads and a squadron of armed police present in case things turned nasty. The entire cost to the county in staging the trial was in excess of $2 million.

The eyes of the world were going to be on the courtroom, it was clear from the start. One wondered how on earth the jury would be able to deliver a clear-eyed verdict in these circumstances. Indeed, on the first day as the jury was selected, many wags joked that it would be a tough job to select a jury of Michael's 'peers'.

How many other people in the world in any way resembled him or lived his peculiar lifestyle? Eventually a jury of twelve was selected, with eight further members in reserve. It was time for the trial to start. District attorney Tom Sneddon – who had pursued an unsuccessful prosecution attempt at Michael in 1993, prompting accusations of a 'vendetta' from the singer's fans – rose to his feet and began his opening statement. He said that Michael had exploited his celebrity to lure Gavin Arvizo to Neverland where he gave him alcoholic drinks, all the better to molest him. Among the specifics were that Michael had shown the thirteen-year-old adult websites, simulated sex with a mannequin in front of him and stood naked in front of the boy. Sneddon, whose speech was interrupted by feedback from the microphone at one point, also outlined the details of the alleged sexual acts.

Bringing his statement to a conclusion, he painted a picture of evil, in stark contrast to how adults normally treated children. 'Instead of reading them *Peter Pan*, Jackson is showing them sexually explicit magazines,' he said with quiet forcefulness. 'Instead of cookies and milk, you can substitute wine, vodka and bourbon.' He summed up the case thus: 'This case is about a conspiracy, it's about the train wreck caused by the Bashir documentary. This is also a case of Michael Jackson's exploitation of a thirteen-year-old boy, a cancer survivor.' In defence, Michael's lawyer Thomas Mesereau was just as confident, saying, 'These charges are fictitious. They are bogus, and they never happened.' He painted unflattering portraits of Michael's accusers and said that 'Neverland is not a haven for criminal activity, a lure for molestation, as characterized by the prosecution. It's a Disneyland-like place, a place for underprivileged and sick children to have a day of fun.' He added that, significantly: 'The children's DNA was never found in Michael Jackson's bedroom after searching and testing. The DNA isn't there because the molestation claims are false.'

As the prosecution case began, *Living with Michael Jackson* was shown to the jurors. During the programme one of his tracks can be heard, and sitting in the courtroom Michael nodded his head along to the music. Bashir repeatedly refused to answer questions and used the Californian 'shield law' which allows journalists to protect their sources. His lawyer repeated: 'Objection, shield law, first amendment,' in response to many of the questions over how he had gone about winning Michael's trust during the making of the documentary. All the same, his appearance prompted fascination. 'The British journalist is coming close to upstaging Jackson himself in what is inevitably being described as the trial of the century,' wrote Ian Herbert in the *Independent*. At the end of that day and the following day, Michael described himself as 'angry' when asked how he felt about the proceedings. Next up was Davellin Arvizo, Gavin's eighteen-year-old sister who said she had seen Michael giving her brother wine at Neverland. She also claimed there was an 'aggressive' atmosphere at the ranch. Referring to the video interview – which was shown to the court – in which the family praised Michael and insisted he had done nothing wrong, she said they were 'coerced' into making it. At the end of the first week of the trial, Michael told reporters he felt things were 'very good'.

He was less positive the following week as he left court and told reporters he could not comment on what had been said in court that day, as he was under 'a gag order'. The day's witness had been Gavin's brother Star, who told the court he had seen Michael molest Gavin on two occasions at Neverland. One time, he said, Michael was masturbating with his right hand while his left hand was in Gavin's underwear. The other time he claimed to have seen Michael licking Gavin's head. Under questioning from the defence, Star admitted to lying during the lawsuit the family brought against JC Penney five years previously. Star's testimony had been a harrowing experience for Michael. As he returned home that evening, he knew that the following day Gavin Arvizo would take to the witness stand.

'I thought he was the coolest guy in the world. He was my best friend ever,' said Gavin the following day when asked how he felt when he first met Michael. He then claimed that Michael had coached him on what to say during the Bashir interview, including suggesting that Gavin tell Bashir that Michael had cured his cancer. During day two of his testimony, Gavin claimed that Michael had masturbated him and fed him wine, vodka and brandy. 'He said not to tell anyone about the Jesus Juice [alcohol] and said this is like a testimony that we'll be friends forever,' said Gavin. He added that his mother was scared the family would be killed if they tried to leave the Neverland ranch. It had been a tough day for Michael's case, which had not been helped by his late arrival in court, wearing pyjamas and slippers. 'He told me he has never experienced such pain in his life,' said spokesperson Raymone Bain of the back pain on which Michael's tardiness had been blamed.

Acting for Michael, Thomas Mesereau was uncompromising in his examination of Gavin. He revealed that the boy had told a teacher that Michael had never molested him. 'It wasn't until you realized that you, your mother, brother and sister weren't going to be a part of Michael Jackson's family that you ever came up with the allegations of molestation, was it?' he suggested to the boy. Gavin replied: 'No, I didn't want to be part of Michael Jackson's family.' Mesereau also documented evidence of Gavin's behavioural problems at school. Gavin said that he denied there had been abuse in his chat with the teacher because he was tired of being teased about his friendship with Michael by classmates. It was an aggressive exchange, with the judge intervening to tell both parties to calm down. Gavin's case was dented further when Police Sergeant Steve Robel said that the boy had been vague about some details of his allegations.

On and on went the examination of the characters of the Arvizo family. Gavin, it was revealed, had once accused comedian George Lopez of stealing $300 from him. Lopez told the court he thought Gavin's father was more interested in making money than helping his son and that he had cut ties with the family after they became too aggressive in their pleas for financial help with Gavin's cancer treatment. When Mr Arvizo had asked Lopez how he should explain his ending the friendship to his son, he replied: 'Tell him his father's an extortionist.' Stan Katz, the psychologist who first interviewed Gavin Arvizo, gave some balance when he told the court that the inconsistencies in the boy's evidence were proof of his honesty. 'Children who make false allegations are usually consistent, almost scripted,' Katz told the court. The pendulum then swung back in Michael's favour when the police admitted they had not found Arvizo's DNA in the singer's bed.

There was considerable damage done to Michael's case when twenty-four-year-old Jason Francia appeared in the witness stand. Francia, the son of a former maid of Michael who had claimed the singer would regularly relieve himself in his clothing and toss the soiled clothes aside, said that the singer had molested him between the ages of seven and ten. He added that he had been haunted by the experience which took him years of counselling to get over. Under cross examination he admitted he had initially told the police that Michael had not molested him. (The matter had eventually ended with an out-of-court settlement between Michael and the Francia family.) Francia's mother then gave evidence saying she had seen Michael showering with another pre-teen boy while she worked for him and that she had further witnessed the singer sleeping with child star Macaualy Culkin. A former guard of Michael made similar allegations but admitted he had sold stories about the alleged abuse to fund a failed lawsuit against the singer for unfair dismissal. Then a chef claimed to have seen Michael fondle Culkin – who would appear later in the case as a defence witness – and Jordan Chandler's mother June appeared to confirm her son had shared a bed with Michael.

Gavin's mother spoke of a flight to Miami the family took with Michael in February 2003. 'That's when I saw Michael licking [Gavin's] head. I thought I was seeing things. I thought it was me,' she said. She also claimed that Michael had told her that Gavin's life was in danger from 'killers' and that the singer held the family against their will at Neverland until they agreed to a filmed interview exonerating Michael. She added that the singer's aides told her that if she 'put Michael in a bad light, that they knew where my parents lived'. Under cross examination she admitted to lying during the lawsuit brought against JC Penney and said of her performance during the video: 'I'm a poor actress.' Michael's barrister countered witheringly, 'Oh, I think you're a good one.' Again, the judge intervened and asked the pair to cool their exchanges.

'Neverland is all about pornography, booze and sex with boys,' said Janet Arvizo – an outburst the judge instructed the jury to ignore. Her five days in the witness stand continued to be dominated by opinionated outbursts, however. 'He's managed to fool the world and I was just one woman inside of that,' she said of Michael. 'What he puts out to the world is not who he really is. Now, because of this criminal case, people know who he really is.' She denied that she faked bruising during her case against JC Penney and also disputed that she had used money raised for Gavin's treatment to pay for her own cosmetic surgery. She had been an unconvincing witness. More convincing was Brian Barron, the former Neverland security guard who appeared to confirm the Arvizos' claim that they had been held against their will. 'We weren't allowed to let him off the property without some sort of permission from the ranch manager,' Mr Barron told the court. Another witness, a travel agent, agreed she had been asked to book one-way tickets for Michael and Gavin to visit Brazil, adding weight to the 'kidnap' claims of the prosecution.

After Michael's ex-wife Debbie Rowe had admitted lying on a video made to defend the star, it was the turn of Los Angeles police detective Rosibel Smith to speak. He claimed that during the raid he had found in a locked cabinet books containing images of naked boys and he read out the inscription, in Michael's handwriting, that he had found inside one of the books: 'Look at the true spirit of happiness and joy in these boys' faces, this is the spirit of boyhood, a life I've never had and will always dream of. This is the life I want for my children.' The prosecution rested its case and the defence filed for an immediate acquittal, arguing the case had not been proven. That was unsuccessful and so the defence case began the following day.

The first defence witnesses were Wade Robson, twenty-two, and Brett Barnes, twenty-three, who had both been regular visitors to Neverland as children. Both flatly denied they had ever been mistreated by Michael. 'I'm telling you, nothing ever happened,' Robson said. Barnes reiterated: 'Never – I wouldn't stand for it.' Previous witnesses claimed to have seen Barnes fondled by the singer – Barnes said they were wrong and he was 'really not happy' about the suggestion. The men's mothers then backed up the evidence, with Ms Barnes saying Michael was 'very pure'. The defence then called a series of Neverland staff past and present who countered the claims of their colleagues who had appeared for the prosecution. The case was going well for Michael but for some onlookers there had yet to be any real excitement in the defence case, particularly as a galaxy of A-list stars had been predicted to give evidence in the singer's favour.

There was a definite frisson, then, on Wednesday 11 May when film star Macaulay Culkin appeared as a witness for the defence. He denied Michael had ever mistreated him during their friend-ship. When it was put to him that abuse may have taken place while he was asleep, Culkin replied: 'I find that unlikely. I think I'd realize that something like that was happening to me.' His evidence was unequivocal, he said firmly: 'I've never seen him do anything improper with anybody.' Michael's former lawyer Mark Geragos was another defence witness. He said of his experiences working for Michael: 'I didn't see anyone doing anything nefarious or criminal.' Quite the contrary, he added: 'I saw someone who was ripe as a target.' Further defence witnesses were called who dented the Arvizos' case that they had been held against their will, and a witness appeared saying he had seen Gavin Arvizo masturbating in front of pornography alone in a room at Neverland. The effect of the latter witness was supposed to show that Arvizo was no innocent, but it might equally have been interpreted as evidence of the ranch being a sexually-charged place.

The trial was coming to an end but not before further defence witnesses threw the Arvizo family's story into doubt. Perhaps most damning was the evidence that Janet Arvizo had spent $7,000 on clothes, cosmetics and meals in restaurants – billed to Michael – during February and March 2003, the same time she claimed she was held captive. Television star Jay Leno and comedian Chris Tucker were the final two witnesses for the defence, both giving accounts of brushes with the Arvizos and painting a picture of Gavin as a very canny, scripted operator. Then, the defence rested. 'You have heard all of the evidence and you will hear the arguments of attorneys,' Judge Melville told the jury on Wednesday 1 June. They would do so on the following day. 'This case is about the exploitation and abuse of a thirteen-year-old cancer survivor at the hands of an international celebrity,' Deputy District Attorney Ron Zonen said for the prosecution. 'The suggestion this was all made up is nonsense,' he added. 'It's unmitigated rubbish. Michael Jackson molested [Gavin Arvizo] and many other boys. That testimony should be believed, and Michael Jackson should be held responsible for what he did.' Then it was time for Thomas Mesereau to sum up the case for the defence. Michael listened intently as the final words that could save him from a prison sentence were spoken by his attorney. 'This is a family where children have been taught to lie,' Mr Mesereau said of the Arvizos. A technical hitch delayed his speech for twenty minutes at one point, but his rousing conclusion was striking. 'This is a family where children have been taught to con. There is no way in the world you can find [the Arvizos] trustworthy beyond reasonable doubt. If you do have the slightest problem and it's a reasonable one, the slightest doubt, and it's a reasonable one, then Mr Jackson must go home and he must be free.'

While the jury were considering their verdict, the media and fan circus continued outside. Relations between the two parties had been far from warm, with many of Michael's fans baiting the press. 'You never report the truth!' they would cry. One fan – a twenty-year-old Knoxville man – was so vociferous that a reporter took out a restraining order against him. Reverend Jesse Jackson appeared again to deliver his latest thoughts to the media who – hungry as ever for a fresh angle – surrounded him with microphones, notebooks and cameras. Another day, Joseph Jackson shoved his way through the media pack to visit Michael at the court – only to be told his son was not there. Michael had been hospitalized the previous day, suffering from dehydration, stress and back pain. 'He's very, very shaky,' said a member of his entourage. 'He's terrified and it's taking a toll on his health.' Finally, on 14 June, the jury was ready to deliver its verdict. Michael arrived that day wearing huge mirrored sunglasses and carrying an umbrella to shield him from the sunlight. He waved to his fans and walked into the courtroom, where due to lack of space only six members of his family would be allowed to watch. The jurors filed back into the court and their demeanour gave nothing away. The judge warned those present that no outbursts would be tolerated – 'no unhappiness or jubilance'.

The verdicts were passed on paper to Judge Melville who maintained a serious expression as he read them. Then the court clerk read out the verdicts, one by one. 'Count one – conspiracy – not guilty,' she said. She then repeated the 'not guilty' verdict for each of the charges. Michael dabbed a tissue to his eyes, Katherine wiped a tear from hers and sister Janet merely stared into the distance. The sound of the crowd outside cheering each verdict could be heard in the courtroom and one fan had released a symbolic white dove when each verdict was announced. Fans were also screaming, crying, releasing balloons and throwing confetti. ('The scenes over here are probably hard to understand for anyone that's not here,' said one British fan outside the court, to global agreement.) Judge Melville then read aloud a statement from the jury: 'We the jury, feeling the weight of the world's eyes upon us, all thoroughly and meticulously studied the testimony, evidence and rules of procedure presented in this court since 31 January 2005. Following the jury instructions, we confidently came to our verdicts. It is out hope that his case is a testament to the belief in our justice system's integrity and truth.' Then, within minutes of the process starting, Michael was hugging and thanking his defence team and strolling out of the courtroom. The 'trial of the century' was over.

Outside the court Mesereau spoke about the case and the effect it had had on Michael. He said: 'Justice was served. Michael Jackson is innocent.' Of Michael's health, he said: '[He] is going to have to go through a period of physical recovery. He's exhausted. He was not sleeping. He was not eating. It was a very, very traumatic experience for him and it's going to take a while for him to recover.' Meanwhile, his opposite number in the case spoke of the well-being of his own client. '[Gavin] was having a difficult time understanding why people wouldn't believe him,' DA Tom Sneddon told NBC. 'It's difficult...to have put his heart and his soul on the line in front of the world and to not be believed.' The world's media had covered the verdict, many television networks interrupting their schedules to report it. Many pundits had been taken by surprise by the outcome. On CNN, the lead defence lawyer from the O. J. Simpson case, Robert Shapiro, had said he expected a guilty verdict, saying the outcome would not have 'Michael Jackson singing "Beat It"'. Another legal insider said confidently: 'I think we're going to see convictions here.' When news of the 'not guilty' verdict came through, Shapiro corrected himself with another play on words: 'Now he's gonna be doing the Moonwalk.' The following morning's edition of the *Sun* echoed Shapiro's pun, with the headline: 'He Beat It.' However, there were harsher words inside. 'An acquittal doesn't clear his name,' the paper said, 'it only muddies the water.' Of the trial itself, the paper wrote: 'There was no sense of good and evil, no sympathetic character to root for. Nearly everyone was dirty, or at the very least, possessed of questionable motives.' The *Daily Mirror* summed up its view of Michael's future with this bleak equation: 'Innocent but tainted forever.'

Naturally, Michael's official website was triumphant – loudly so. Visitors to it that day found the word 'Innocent' displayed alongside the 'V for victory' sign as victorious music played from their computers' speakers. The website then compared the occasion of his acquittal with other historic dates such as the birth of Martin Luther King and the release of Nelson Mandela. Perspective was being lost. As for Michael himself, despite reports that he was exhausted and sick, he was actually in the recording studio the day after he was acquitted. A new studio had been built in the grounds of Neverland, funded by Sheikh Abdullah bin Hamad Al Khalifa, the twenty-nine-year-old son of the king of Bahrain who hoped to pursue his dreams of a career in pop via his new association with Michael. He had given millions of dollars to Michael to help him with legal fees and now hoped the singer would record a single for him. However, Michael was unhappy at the ranch, which he felt was 'no longer a home' after the police investigation which had 'violated' the property.

Two weeks after the case ended – after problems retrieving his passport from the authorities – Michael flew to Bahrain with his children at his side. There, he hoped, he could find some solace, recharge his batteries and pick up the pieces of his life. He and the sheikh discussed ambitious plans including their own record label for which Michael would record two albums, a new autobiography and a live performance. None came to fruition and the sheikh later took legal action against Michael to recover the money which he had invested in the projects and to fund Michael's lifestyle in Bahrain. Michael settled out of court for a huge sum. In the meantime, Michael had really enjoyed life in Bahrain. It was not his first visit – his brother Jermaine had a home there and had converted to Islam in 1989. Much of Michael's behaviour raised eyebrows among the locals. One cleric slammed Michael as 'effeminate', an accusation the singer was doing little to dispel. He was spotted in the women's toilets of a shopping centre applying make-up and was also often seen wearing women's clothes, including a full-length dress, complete with veil. Michael's love of dressing up and his fondness for disguises was a long-running affair, but he was risking huge offence to the locals with his behaviour in Bahrain. Despite this, there was soon speculation that he might convert to Islam. 'I think it is most probable,' his brother Jermaine told the *Daily Telegraph*. 'He could do so much, just like I am trying to do. Michael and I and the word of God, we could do so much.' He was also sighted during a visit to St Tropez wearing a woman's sunhat and high heels.

In the meantime, having fallen out with the sheikh, Michael swapped Bahrain for Berkshire, where he stayed in the historic stately home Cliveden for a week. Charlie Chaplin, Winston Churchill, Harold Macmillan and Christine Keeler had also stayed there in the past and when Michael left at the end of the week he had run up a £30,000 bill. He had enjoyed his stay and tried – unsuccessfully – to buy the property. He was soon living in various locations in Ireland, including the expensive Luggala Lodge on the shores of Lough Tay, and in a lodge in County Westmeath. He found peace there, eating breakfast with his children each morning and then walking to a recording studio where he was recording with Black Eyed Peas singer Will.i.am. His recording colleague was impressed with Michael. 'He's awesome,' Will.i.am told *Q* magazine. 'That guy is smart. Really analytical and a perfectionist. That's why it takes so long for him to finish stuff.' He added that Michael's ambitions for the new material were grand. 'He said, "You know, I just wanna make unprecedented music! I just wanna shock 'em! Wanna go for the jugular! Aim for the throat!"'

He had fallen short of going for the jugular when he appeared at the World Music Awards at London's Earls Court in November 2006. This was to be his first live performance in nine years and expectations were sky-high. It was an evening of disappointments: host Lindsay Lohan fluffed her lines and then there was an agonizing half-hour delay following Beyoncé's performance. Michael took to the stage to a hysterical reaction to accept his lifetime achievement award but then promptly left, to be replaced by singer Rihanna, who was loudly booed by Michael's fans, disappointed he had not performed. He did later in the night – but half-heartedly to say the least. A children's choir sang 'We Are the World', and Michael joined them briefly to sing just two lines, before leaving the stage. Boos once more filled the cavernous venue. His next public appearance was at the funeral of soul legend James Brown in Georgia in December 2006. There, Michael kissed the body of the man who he had been compared with since childhood. Some observers said Michael looked as much of a corpse as Brown.

He soon fulfilled Jermaine's prediction and reportedly converted to Islam, while at a friend's mansion in Los Angeles. With Yusuf

Islam (or Cat Stevens, as he was known until his own conversion) watching admiringly, an imam took Michael through the shahada, the Muslim declaration of belief. As a result of the conversion, it was said, he was known as Mikaael, the name of one of Allah's angels. He was said to have rejected the name Mustafa, which means 'the chosen one'. Becoming a Muslim was a big change in the life of the boy who had previously been a Jehovah's Witness and was rumoured in some quarters to be homosexual. Although the reports of his conversion were never definitively confirmed, Jermaine added to the suspicion when he said after his brother's death: 'Allah be with you, Michael, always. I love you.'

Returning to the music, in his conversations with Will.i.am back at the recording studio, Michael had also said he was aiming for 'international number-ones' with his new material. He could certainly have done with the money. One of the biggest surprises of Michael's latter years was the way the most successful entertainer of all time, who had sold 750 million records, found himself in such colossal debt. How could this happen? The story began to unravel during his 2005 trial, in which prosecutors had described him as a 'spendaholic' who had a 'billionaire spending habit for only a millionaire's spending budget'. His spending had exceeded his income for decades, and an accountant gave evidence that the annual deficit was up to $30 million. Michael's annual income was estimated to be around $12 million by the time of the trial, most of which came from the royalties generated by his own songs and the 50 per cent share of The Beatles' back catalogue which he had acquired in the 1980s. However, his Neverland ranch cost $5 million a year to maintain, while his spendthrift nature and the countless legal actions he faced, from everyone from disgruntled former employees to vets, soon pushed him into debts of around $400 million. This problem had also been exacerbated by his *laissez faire* attitude to his finances. He regularly changed financial managers and was said by an unnamed aide to have 'a screaming fit' when sensible advice was offered to him. One report estimated that he had spent $1 billion in two decades.

* * *

His transactions and decisions during the final years of his life tell a tale of a man in desperation and bewilderment over his financial affairs. On the advice of his unofficial manager Tohme R. Tohme, he hired Los Angeles-based auctioneer Darren Julien to grab the plentiful valuables from Neverland and sell them to fans. A total of ten lorries' worth of such gold-dust memorabilia – including a gilded throne, sequined gloves, antique pianos and even the famous Neverland gates – was collected and prepared for auction. Months later, Michael had an abrupt – and not uncharacteristic – change of heart and launched a lawsuit against Julien. 'He was launching a lawsuit to stop us doing the thing he had contracted us to do,' Julien told *Q* magazine. Michael was also threatened with repossession of Neverland as he defaulted on debt repayments. It was against this background of growing debt, desperation and disorder that Michael agreed to perform comeback concerts.

He had first been approached in 2007 about staging a comeback. Randy Phillips, chief executive of concert promoter AEG Live, who had arranged a successful set of concerts at London's O2 arena, was the man who put the proposal to Michael. 'We were flatly turned down,' Phillips told *Q* magazine. But then, in 2008, Michael had a change of heart and met with Phillips to discuss a series of shows. What was agreed later became the subject of contention, but Phillips says of the singer's demeanour at the meeting, 'He didn't seem frail. He seemed emotionally, physically and mentally ready.' He later restated this impression, telling a Channel 4 documentary: 'I would trade my body for [Jackson's] tomorrow, he's in fantastic shape.' Everyone was agreed that Michael would perform some comeback shows, and an announcement in London for the dates was arranged. The world's press would be invited, as would thousands of excited fans.

Michael arrived at the press conference characteristically late, but his lateness did nothing to quell the hysterical joy of the fans who were present. 'This is it,' he told the assembled media and fans. 'I just want to say these will be my final performances in London. This is it, when I say this is it, this is it,' he added. 'I'll be performing the songs my fans want to hear – this is it. This is really it. This is the final curtain call. I'll see you in July.' The first date of the officially named 'This Is It' shows was scheduled for 8 July, and within minutes of the announcement bookmakers were taking bets that he would not fulfil a single one of the ten gigs he announced. The likelihood of this increased in the eyes of some when the dates were subsequently rearranged and when news broke that Michael had only attended two of the forty-five rehearsals. However, far from being cancelled, the total dates arranged were actually increased from ten to fifty, with Michael claiming he never agreed to the increase. 'I don't know how I'm going to do fifty shows,' he told fans outside the studio where he was rehearsing for the dates. 'I'm not a big eater – I need to put some weight on. I went to bed knowing I sold ten dates and woke up to the news I was booked to do fifty.' He would therefore perform in front of 800,000 fans.

After his death, this issue became highly contentious as certain people from Michael's camp firmly and angrily stated that he had never agreed to fifty shows. 'Michael only agreed to ten shows,' his father told ABC news. 'Then they went and added all these shows. I was worried about his health because...no artist can do all those shows, back-to-back like that. I knew Michael couldn't do all those shows without a rest in between.' Michael's legal adviser Leonard Rowe backed up Joseph's words. 'MJ told me himself that he never wanted to do fifty shows, he only wanted to do ten,' he said. Randy Phillips countered, insisting that it had been Michael's idea to increase the original run of concerts to fifty, saying that because of how the dates were arranged, the singer would not have been doing the shows back-to-back but would have been averaging fewer than three shows a week. 'If *that* was too many, then one would have been too many,' he said.

Accounts of the state of Michael's health in his final days vary wildly. Certainly the picture painted by one man who saw him at what proved to be his final rehearsal is of a man still capable of putting on a show. We hear of a man in fine health, and charged with enthusiasm about the actual shows to come. He reportedly stormed onto the stage and shouted to the assembled dancers and musicians: 'Come on, let's make this happen!' During the rehearsal he ran through twelve songs in total. At one point he said: 'This is me. The true me. I feel so alive. I feel as though I want to perform forever.' Photographer Kevin Mazur told the *Daily Mirror*: 'Between songs, he burst into laughter and joked around with his dancers and the director.' Added Mazur: 'I have never seen him so happy. But there was a cool professionalism about him. He was there to do a job and, boy, did he do it well. It was incredible.' Perhaps the most poignant moment came when Michael turned to Mazur and said: 'This is where I belong. Why oh why have I left it so long?' He *had* left it too long – hours later he was dead.

* * *

After a late night – the rehearsal reportedly went on until around 1 a.m. and Michael waved to fans outside the venue as he left – he was still in bed late into the morning of the following day. His home at this stage was a vast, $100,000 a month mansion in the plush environs of Holmby Hills. Much of what happened in the minutes and hours that followed remains the subject of fierce disagreement and is clouded in controversy. Some claim he was given an injection of the painkiller Demerol, others dispute this. Michael's personal doctor Conrad Murray had only worked for the singer for thirteen days. He says he discovered him unable to breathe but still with a faint pulse. Paramedics were called to the singer's home after an emergency call was made while Dr Murray performed CPR on the singer. They paramedics arrived quickly, a little over three minutes after the call. The monitor in the ambulance simply read 'Fifty-year-old male – not breathing at all'. They rushed him to the UCLA medical centre, pumping oxygen into his lungs during the journey and trying to massage his heart back into action. He was wheeled in at speed and one of his entourage shouted at nurses to 'Do everything,' adding, 'You've got to save him! You've got to save him!' However, according to one nurse, it was clear on his arrival that it was too late to save him.

At 2.26 p.m., Michael Jackson was dead.

* * *

Michael's manager Frank DiLeo had been at his client's side in the hospital and after signing the paperwork for the coroner's office, he was faced with an onerous task. He walked down the hospital corridor and entered the small room where Michael's three children anxiously awaited news with his mother Katherine – Joseph, in Las Vegas, was in telephone contact with the hospital. DiLeo shook his head as he tried to find the right words to tell the children their father had died. He took a deep breath, and said: 'I'm sorry, children, your father has passed away.' There was a moment of silence before Paris screamed: 'No, no, Daddy. No, no!' Katherine had already feared the worst, but was also absolutely devastated at the death of her son. 'I have lost my baby Michael,' she said. 'He was a good boy, no matter what they say about him.'

For the world's media, the death of Michael Jackson was of course an absolutely colossal story. The first to report the news had been the American celebrity website TMZ, just eighteen minutes after Michael died. The *Los Angeles Times* website was next, seven minutes later, and then the rest of the world's media leapt. Both websites crashed under the weight of sudden traffic and Google received so many searches for 'Michael Jackson' it at first assumed it was under attack from a virus. Television networks interrupted their schedules to break the news of Michael's death, which dominated rolling news for days on end. In the following days, newspapers and magazines published commemorative editions.

Naturally, just as much of the coverage of Michael in life had been outlandish, so 'out of this world' stories emerged following his death. Perhaps it was fitting that the man known for his Moonwalk dance move, who named his autobiography *Moonwalker*, would have a crater on the moon named after him. The Lunar Republic Society revealed this tribute, which Michael would surely have appreciated. "The official designation of a lunar crater is a singular honour bestowed upon only a select few luminaries,' said a spokesman for the society. 'Among those receiving this rare tribute over the past century are Leonardo da Vinci, Christopher Columbus, Sir Isaac Newton, Julius Caesar and Jules Verne.' This was just one of miles of column inches devoted to Michael in the wake of his death. It felt as though this had been one of the biggest celebrity news stories in living memory as our television screens, newspapers and magazines were bombarded with and dominated by Jackson-related news. The same was true of the worldwide web. Soon, research by Global Language Monitor (GLM) found that Michael Jackson's death was the second most covered story on the internet of the twenty-first century. Only the election of President Barack Obama received more coverage, GLM found. This meant that Michael's death received more online coverage than the Iraq War, 9/11, the global financial meltdown, the Beijing Olympics, Hurricane Katrina, the death of Pope John Paul II and the 2004 tsunami. It was remarkable: even in death Michael was proving a record-breaking sensation.

* * *

So what killed Michael Jackson? Reports in the weeks following his death came up with no end of theories: he had died of a drug overdose after years abusing prescription drugs with his arms covered in track marks, he had committed suicide, he was murdered. Some even speculated that he was alive and well, having faked his own death to increase record sales. Other theorists postulated that he had in fact been dead for decades, buried at Neverland, and that an impostor had been impersonating him ever since. True, these are outlandish theories, the stuff of internet lunacy. But given the eccentric way he lived his life, Michael was always going to spark 'wacko' stories after his death. Do not expect to hear the last of these theories for a while. Even once official investigations are concluded it is likely that many will never accept their results – over thirty years after the death of Elvis Presley, people still speculate that he is alive and conspiracy theories still surround the deaths of other iconic figures like John F. Kennedy and Diana, Princess of Wales.

As the speculation over Michael's death, and the state of his health in his final months, mounted it was easy to lose sight of the facts. Soon after Michael's death a coroner's spokesperson announced the preliminary autopsy results, saying there were no signs of foul play or trauma to Michael's body. However, no conclusive cause of Michael's death was offered as the full autopsy continued, as did reports suggesting he had been addicted to the painkiller Demerol for twenty years. 'Everybody around him knew about it,' his video producer Marc Schaffel said on ABC of the addiction rumour. 'He didn't advertise it to the world, but anybody in his inner circle knew.' Such reports are given some credence when considered in the light of the lyrics of Michael's song 'Morphine', released in 1997: 'Kick in the back baby; A heart-attack baby,' followed by the chant, 'Demerol, Demerol; Oh God he's taking Demerol.' These lyrics seem, in retrospect, haunting.

Reports of the state of Michael's health in his last years varied wildly. John Wright worked on what is believed to be the final authorized photo shoot with Michael, in 2007, for Guinness World Records. 'I want to make it clear,' Wright told Q magazine. 'He was attentive, he was focused, he was having fun. That wasn't an ill man who was in the room with me.' As we have seen, even up to his final full day alive, Michael is reported by some as being a picture of health. 'He was totally there – a hundred per cent there in fact,' photographer Kevin Mazur told the *Mirror*. 'You would never suspect this would have ever happened – especially after his performance on stage.' Others paint an entirely different portrait of his performance at the rehearsals for his 'This Is It' dates, saying Michael was 'listless' and lethargic. 'He was frail, you might say,' Patrick Woodroffe, a lighting director, told the *Daily Telegraph*.

J. Randy Taraborrelli used the same language. He said Michael had become 'very frail, totally, totally underweight'. Some go even further, saying that in his final months Michael was a sickened and broken man – as frail as a pensioner. Celebrity blogger Ian Halperin, who also wrote a controversial book called *Unmasked: The Final Years of Michael Jackson*, posted an online article in December 2008 saying Michael had a life-threatening disease called Alpha One, a genetic lung condition. Halperin was quoted by *In Touch* magazine as saying he believed Michael 'had six months to live' and photographs of a frail Michael, wearing a surgical mask and being pushed in a wheelchair, hardly detracted from the blogger's claim. Michael's camp denied the report. Six months and one day later, Michael died. Halperin also claims that during the final months of his life, a suffering Michael called Paris to his bedside and told her that he did not expect to live for long. On 21 June, just days before he died, Michael reportedly told an aide: 'It's not working out. I'm better off dead. I don't have anywhere left to turn. I'm done.' Other claims from Halperin are that in the final months of his life Michael was terrified he would not be able to perform at the upcoming concerts and that he was barely eating or sleeping. Indeed, writes Halperin, even when he did manage to sleep he was plagued with nightmares, including one that he would be murdered.

Then, of course, there was the question of his ever-changing facial appearance. He had long claimed that he suffered from the condition vitiligo, which destroys skin pigmentation, as a result of a gene passed on by his father. 'It is something I cannot help,' he said, adding that he was 'proud to be a black American' and would not bleach his skin. Many doctors did not believe him, not least because vitiligo is a genetic condition and none of his siblings seem affected. Many observers speculated that as well as numerous nose jobs and the cleft he had put into his chin, he also had a forehead lift, a cheekbone operation and had his lips and eyelids thinned out. One estimate says that by 1990 he had already undergone ten cosmetic surgery operations and it is true that his nose had dramatically changed shape by this time, taking on an almost pixie shape. However, he continued to deny any cosmetic surgery and in 1992 launched a lawsuit against the *Daily Mirror*, which had claimed he was 'hideously disfigured' by such work, and that it had left him a 'scarred phantom'. An out-of-court settlement was later reached by Michael and the newspaper, which apologized to the singer. Still, the work appeared to continue, with cheek implants seemingly inserted in 1995 and his eyes apparently widening in 2002. By the time of his death, some observers said that his nose was on the brink of collapse and it was reported that surgeons had been forced to use cartilage from his ear in an attempt to save it.

There are no signs of a consensus forming over the question of Michael's overall health in his final years, nor about the question of the nature of his relationships with children. His death robs us of the chance of bringing the matter to closure or conclusion. In the weeks after Michael's death, Halperin revealed that he had personally interviewed forty-two adults who – as children – had stayed the night at Neverland. All denied that Michael had behaved inappropriately with them. 'There was nothing like that,' one told the biographer. 'Michael was just this big oversized goofy kid.' Another said: 'I may have spent more time with him than anyone else. No way is [he] a child abuser. Take it from me.' Halperin notes that studies claim that the average child abuser amasses more than a hundred victims in their lifetime – why, he asks, did more not come forward? Significantly, Halperin – who admits he set out to 'nail' Michael – uncovered further evidence that points to his innocence, including suggestions that Michael settled with the Chandlers under duress from his insurers. However, people continued to suspect Michael of wrongdoing in the wake of his death, asking why the world was so mourning a man accused of child abuse. The suspicion will never entirely be dispelled.

As these controversies played out across the world's media, plans had been made for the day of Michael's funeral. It would be a two-part affair, starting with a private funeral attended just by his family. This would be followed by a memorial service, which was to be held at the Staples Center arena in downtown Los Angeles, where Michael had been rehearsing for the O2 concerts. The day was to have a commercial air: the sixteen-vehicle Jackson family motorcade was sponsored (by Range Rover) and the *Guardian* newspaper described 'really rather copious branding for Staples' at the Center, which seemed inappropriate for such an occasion. Some 3,200 Los Angeles police were on duty in the area. The Federal Aviation Administration approved a temporary flight ban for a mile around the venue, below 2,500 feet, for fear of an influx of helicopters. It was certainly a spectacular event, and an estimated global audience of a billion watched it unfold. Television networks cleared their schedules for the memorial, affording it the sort of importance normally given to royal weddings. Spontaneous public gatherings happened in Harlem and Times Square in New York, as well as in Gary, Indiana, where Michael was born and raised.

The Jackson family left Joseph and Katherine's Encino home at 8.03 a.m. and drove to the Forest Lawn Cemetery in Hollywood Hills for the funeral at the Hall of Liberty chapel. Meanwhile, eleven Asian elephants were escorted into the Staples Center, ahead of the Ringling Bros circus show that was to be held in the venue the following day. At 8.30 a.m., the two hundred or so mourners at the Forest Lawn Cemetery attended the private funeral. Thirty minutes later they emerged and filed into the motorcade once more. Michael's bronze- and gold-plated coffin was carried into a hearse, and his mother Katherine accompanied it for the twenty-five minute drive to the Staples Center. There, an estimated crowd of more than five thousand fans stood as close to the Center as they were allowed. One group had travelled three days to be there. Some had sold precious personal belongings to fund their trip, which ended with them standing behind a police barrier. Not everyone was there to pay their respects. A small group of protestors – fewer than ten – stood with placards decrying Michael. They read 'Jacko in Hell', 'You're Going to Hell' and 'Mourn for Your Sins'. The cost of policing the event and its surroundings was enormous, to the degree that the mayor of Los Angeles, Antonio Villaraigosa, had appealed to Jackson fans to contribute to the bill via the internet payment website PayPal.

The 17,500 fans who had won tickets to the memorial through a lottery took their seats in the Staples Center and were handed a gold-covered programme which included photographs of Michael with Nelson Mandela, Bill Clinton and Ronald Reagan, and quotes from friends and family. One, from Tito, read: 'I watched the light in Michael's eyes fade as he faced trials and tribulations for being misunderstood.' The ceremony started at 10.30 a.m., half an hour later than originally planned, with a gospel choir singing Andrae Crouch's 'Soon and Very Soon'. Meanwhile, Michael's coffin, covered in red roses, was carried by his brothers and presented centre-stage as the choir sang, 'We are going to see the king.' There was a message of condolence from Nelson Mandela. Michael was a 'giant and a legend' said the former president of South Africa. 'We remember this man by celebrating all of the love he brought to all of our lives for half a century,' said Pastor Lucious Smith. 'Our hearts are heavy today because [he] is gone far too soon, but as long as we remember our time with him, the truth is he is never really gone at all.' Through his words and music, Smith said, 'Michael did so much to try and heal our world.' Then pop royalty Mariah Carey took to the stage to sing 'I'll Be There'. Behind her on the screens ran a montage of photographs of Michael as a child. Already emotions were running high among those present, and many of the millions watching on television around the world.

From one pop diva to another, after Carey came Queen Latifah. 'I'm here representing millions of fans around the world who grew up listening to Michael, being inspired and loving Michael from a distance,' she said. 'Somehow when Michael Jackson sang and when he danced...we felt he was right there. He made you believe in yourself.' After these heartfelt words, Latifah read a poem by Maya Angelou. Next was Lionel Richie, who had co-written the song 'We Are the World' with Michael in the 1980s, wearing a yellow flower in his buttonhole. Richie said: 'In Birmingham, Alabama, and Birmingham, England, we are missing Michael Jackson. But we do know that we had him.' He then sang 'Jesus Is Love', a Commodores song.

Twenty-five minutes into the memorial, Berry Gordy, founder of Motown, took to the stage to deliver his own thoughts. 'Michael Jackson went into orbit and never came down,' he said. 'Though it ended way too soon, Michael's life was beautiful.' Gordy recalled the Jackson brothers' first audition for the label, in 1968. Speaking as if he was present that day – whereas he actually watched the audition later on video – he said of Jackson: 'This little kid had an incredible knowingness about him...he sung a Smokey Robinson song called "Who's Lovin' You". He sang it with the sadness and passion of a man who'd been living the blues and heartbreak his whole life. And as great as Smokey sang it, I thought Michael was better.' In the audience, Robinson himself chuckled in modest agreement with Gordy's assessment.

Berry Gordy was the first speaker to make any reference to some of the controversies of Michael's life, saying, 'Sure, there were some sad, sad times, and maybe some questionable decisions on his part, but Michael Jackson accomplished everything he dreamed of.' (Later in the ceremony, Texan congresswoman Sheila Jackson Lee also touched on the saga: 'We understand laws, and we know that people are innocent until proven otherwise. That is what the Constitution stands for.') However, Gordy was quickly back on easier terrain, and the rousing conclusion of his speech brought the loudest acclaim from the audience thus far. 'The more I think about Michael Jackson, the more I think the King of Pop is not big enough for him,' he said. 'I think he is simply the greatest entertainer that ever lived...Michael, thank you.' There then followed more footage on the big screens, a compilation of Michael's pop videos and footage of some of his most spectacular live performances. It was another reminder of the iconic brilliance of his career at its peak. In his day he had been peerless.

Michael's sometime Motown colleague Stevie Wonder said, 'This is a moment that I wished that I didn't have to see coming. But I do know that God is good, and I do know that as much as we may feel that we need Michael here with us, God must have needed him far more.' With true showman class he then sang 'Never Dreamed You'd Leave in the Summer'. He was followed by sportsmen Kobe Bryant and Magic Johnson, who recalled visiting Michael and eating grilled chicken while the singer consumed Kentucky Fried Chicken, rating this experience as the 'greatest moment in my life'. On a less bizarre note, he concluded: 'His three children will have the most incredible grandmother that God has put on this earth...so may God continue to bless this incredible family. We're praying for you. Remain strong.' The sportsmen were followed by *American Idol* star Jennifer Hudson, who sang 'Will You Be There'.

After the humorous moments of Magic Johnson's speech, came a more sombre orator, Reverend Al Sharpton. 'I first met Michael around 1970,' he recalled. 'From that day as a cute kid to this moment, he never gave up dreaming. It was that dream that changed culture all over the world. When Michael started, it was a different world. But because Michael kept going, because he didn't accept limitations, because he refused to let people decide his boundaries, he opened up the whole world.' The reverend then put Michael's career into perspective and concluded with a heartfelt plea to Michael's children. 'He put on one glove, pulled his pants up and broke down the colour curtain. When now our videos are shown and magazines put us on the cover, it was Michael Jackson that brought blacks and whites and Asians and Latinos together. Michael made us love each other. I want his three children to know, there wasn't nothing strange about your daddy. It was strange what your daddy had to deal with. He dealt with it anyway. He dealt with it for us.' A statement from the absent Diana Ross was delivered. 'I'm trying to find closure, I want you to know that even though I am not there at the Staples Center I am there in my heart,' said the woman Michael had been so obsessed with during his childhood. 'I've decided to pause and be silent. This feels right for me. Michael was a personal love of mine, a treasured part of my world, part of the fabric of my life in a way that I can't seem to find words to express.'

After a musical interlude from John Mayer, Michael's friend Brooke Shields was next to contribute. Her relationship with Michael had been much speculated on in the past, she acknowledged, and often referred to in disparaging terms. 'But to us it was the most natural and easiest of friendships,' she said, 'maybe it was because we both understood what it was like to be in the spotlight from a very young age. Both of us needed to be adults very early. But when we were together, we were two little kids having fun.' It was one of the memorial's more specific and personal tributes. Delivering it had been difficult for Shields, who broke down regularly during her speech. Michael's brother Jermaine then sang a Charlie Chaplin song, 'Smile'. Like the rest of the official funeral party, he was wearing a single, white, sequinned glove in tribute to the unique style of his departed brother. Martin Luther King's children, Martin Luther King III and Bernice King, made their own spoken contributions, with the latter saying: 'At the end of the day, it is only God's love that will sustain you and move you to a higher ground, far above the noise of life.' It was then time for more music, as Usher sang the song that said it all for Michael's fans: 'Gone Too Soon'.

After footage of the ten-year-old Michael singing Smokey Robinson's 'Who's Lovin' You' was shown, Robinson himself took his turn to speak. He said he could not believe that Michael was only ten years of age when he so brilliantly sang the lyrics of hurt and pain that only an adult should be able to understand fully. Concluded the singer: 'My brother is in a place now where he is most certainly going to live forever. But he's going to live forever twice, because he's going to live forever right here: the world will never, ever forget Michael Jackson.' The next to sing on the stage was – to the surprise of some observers – Shaheen Jafargholi, the twewlve-year-old contestant from British reality television show *Britain's Got Talent*. His presence there confused many but was explained by the family, who said that Michael had been impressed by Jafargholi's performance on the show which he had watched on website YouTube. The youngster, who had been scheduled to perform at each of the fifty O2 concerts, said it was a 'mind-blowing' honour to sing at the memorial.

A star-studded ensemble sang 'We Are the World', the song Michael had co-written for a charity single to bring aid to the starving of Africa. The line 'there are people dying' took on a personal resonance that Michael could never have foreseen when he wrote it during the 1980s. The remainder of the service was taken up by moving personal tributes from Michael's family. His brother Marlon recalled the peculiar nature of their childhood. He said: 'I will treasure the good times, the fun we had, singing, dancing, laughing. I remember when we used to come home from school and grab a quick bite to eat and try to watch *The Three Stooges* – as much of it as possible before Mother would come in and say it's time to go to the recording studio.'

He then told a story which drew laughter from many. 'I also

remember a time when I went into the record store,' he said. 'There was this man purchasing a lot of CDs. He was an older gentleman, he had a short afro, bucked, crooked teeth and his clothes were rumpled. I walked up behind him and said, "Michael, what are you doing in this store?" I told him, "Michael, you're my brother, I can spot you anywhere regardless of your make-up."' Bringing his speech to an end, he spoke of how the level of Michael's fame must have affected his life. 'We will never, never understand what he endured,' he said adamantly. 'Not being able to walk across the street without a crowd gathered around, being judged, being ridiculed. How much pain can one take? Maybe now, Michael, they will leave you alone.'

The memorial was drawing to an end but was about to witness its most memorable and most discussed contribution. Michael's daughter Paris was a surprise speaker for many watching. Michael had gone to great lengths during his life to keep his children hidden from public view, so this was the first time the world at large heard the voice of any of his offspring. What Paris had to say was emotionally charged. 'I just wanted to say, ever since I was born, Daddy has been the best father you could ever imagine,' she said, her voice wavering. 'And I just wanted to say I love him so much.' It was a raw moment and one that would be discussed widely for days across the globe. Indeed, testament to Michael's celebrity was the way that every minute of the ceremony was dissected around the world online and in everyday conversations.

Matthew Price of the BBC summed up the memorial with honesty and fairness. 'It could have been so tacky, based on some of the events of the previous twelve days,' he said. 'But this was a very personal public ceremony. There were moments of humour, moments of sadness. But it was a celebration that surely, whatever you think of him, was worthy of such a global star.' Outside the venue, the initials 'MJ' were written in the sky by an aeroplane, to applause. It had been an incredible send-off for an incredible man. Meanwhile, the coffin was taken away but not for immediate burial at Forest Lawn as many suspected. The coroners were still examining Michael's brain and the family insisted that he would not be buried without it. Just as Michael's body continued to wait to be laid to rest, so did the question of exactly how he died. Police Chief William Bratton told CNN that police were awaiting toxicology results. 'Are we dealing with a homicide or are we dealing with accidental overdose...I don't have that information.' In the weeks that followed, speculation that Michael had been murdered continued, including from his sister LaToya.

Later in the week, fans gathered in Gary, Indiana to honour his memory at the place of his birth and upbringing. 'This is the origin of it all,' civil-rights leader Jesse Jackson told a 6,000-strong crowd who joined the event at a local baseball ground. 'This is where Michael learned to dance, where he learned to sing, where he learned to sacrifice.' What would the boy who grew up there make of the man he became and the legacy he left behind after his untimely death? Could he ever have dreamed of the successes and controversies to come? Given the level of mourning that greeted his death, it seems that the memory of the successes will far outlive that of the controversies. It is Michael's music that will be his ultimate legacy and his astonishingly fantastic songs – which were the soundtrack to the lives of millions – will continue to be loved for generations to come. 'If you enter this world knowing you are loved and leave this world knowing the same, then everything that happened in between can be dealt with,' he once said. The music of Michael Jackson will be loved forever and in that sense, his legend lives on forever.

CHAPTER SEVEN

In the hours and days after Michael passed away, those who knew, admired and loved him paid emotional tributes to him as an artist, friend and man. Here is a selection of those tributes…

'I can't stop crying over the sad news. I have always admired Michael Jackson. The world has lost one of the greats but his music will live on forever.'

— Madonna

'I loved Michael with all my soul and I can't imagine life without him. We had so much in common and we had such loving fun together. I still can't believe it. I don't want to believe it. My life feels so empty. I don't think anyone knew how much we loved each other. The purest, most giving love I've known. Oh God! I'm going to miss him. I can't yet imagine life without him. But I guess with God's help, I'll learn. I keep looking at the photo he gave me which says, "To my true love Elizabeth, I love you for ever". And, I will love him for ever.'

— Elizabeth Taylor

'He broke barriers and he changed radio formats. With music, he made it possible for people like Oprah Winfrey and Barack Obama to impact the mainstream world. His legacy is unparalleled. Michael Jackson will never be forgotten.'
                                                                    – Usher

'We went back about thirty-five years. Michael Jackson made culture accept a person of colour way before Tiger Woods, way before Oprah Winfrey, way before Barack Obama. Michael did with music what they did in sports, in politics, and in television. No controversy will erase the historic impact. Michael Jackson was a trailblazer. He was a historic figure that people will measure music and the industry by.'
                                                      – Reverend Al Sharpton

'There are certain people in our popular culture that just capture people's imaginations. And in death, they become even larger.'
                                                          – Barack Obama

'When I think of him, I think of this young boy, this teenager I first met. He was a great teenager, optimistic and adorable. I'm having a million different reactions I didn't expect I would feel. He was a great singer – God gives you certain gifts, and this child was just an extraordinary child touched by this ability. He could sing like nobody else and he was able to connect with people.'   – Cher

'Michael Jackson showed me that you can actually see the beat. He made the music come to life. He made me believe in magic. I will miss him.'
                                                              – P. Diddy

'I am shocked. I am overwhelmed by this tragedy. Michael Jackson has been an idol for me all my life. He was not only a talented person, but he was unique – a genius. It's such a loss. It feels like when Kennedy died, when Elvis died. My sympathy goes to the family. It's a big loss and it's not even sinking in right now.'

– Celine Dion

'He's the most misunderstood man in the world. Everyone thought he was this weird freak, but when you're with him he's as normal as everyone else. The guy had a good heart and would do everything he can, but everyone looking in couldn't understand him.'

– Jackson's former bodyguard Matt Fiddes

'The incomparable Michael Jackson has made a bigger impact on music than any other artist in the history of music. He was magic. He was what we all strive to be…I love you Michael.'

– Beyoncé Knowles

'He has been an inspiration throughout my entire life and I'm devastated he's gone.'

– Britney Spears

'We have lost a genius and a true ambassador of not only pop music but of all music. He has been an inspiration to multiple generations and I will always cherish the moments I shared with him on stage and all of the things I learned about music from him and the time we spent together.'

– Justin Timberlake

'I feel privileged to have hung out and worked with Michael. He was a massively talented boy-man with a gentle soul. His music will be remembered forever and my memories of our time together will be happy ones.'   – Sir Paul McCartney

'Michael Jackson was easily as influential as James Brown, and that's saying a lot. He was the Fred Astaire of his time.'   – Alice Cooper

'He was an extraordinary friend, artist and contributor to the world. I join his family and his fans in celebrating his incredible life and mourning his untimely passing.'   – Brooke Shields

'He was a kind, genuine and wonderful man. He was also one of the greatest entertainers that ever lived. I loved him very much and I will miss him every remaining day of my life.'   – Liza Minnelli

'Let us remember him for his unparalleled contribution to the world of music, his generosity of spirit in his quest to heal the world, and the joy he brought to his millions of devoted fans throughout the world. I feel blessed to have performed with him several times and to call him my friend. No artist will ever take his place. His star will shine forever.'   – Mariah Carey

'His legacy in music will always be remembered, but a lot of people don't know what a fun and kind guy he was. I think Michael would be smiling right now knowing what an amazing legacy he left.'
                                        – Jimmy Osmond

'I'm absolutely devastated at this news. I just don't have the words. Divinity brought our souls together and allowed us to do what we could do through the 80s. To this day that music is played in every corner of the world, and the reason is because he had it all – talent, grace and professionalism. I've lost my little brother today and part of my soul has gone with him.'

– Quincy Jones

'There will never be another talent like Michael Jackson. He was the first live performer I ever saw. I got to see him at Madison Square Garden when I was eight. If not for him, I wouldn't be doing what I'm doing. He gave me joy as a child and showed me the way to go. He was music, period. May you rest in peace, sweet Michael. You gave us all you had to give.'

– Lenny Kravitz

'I've known Michael for many years and we've done many different things together over the years. I know his family and it's just a total shock. I will personally miss him, I will miss his light, I will miss his star, I will miss who he has caused other people to become because of his greatness. He upped the standard.'

– Donna Summer

'I am so very sad and confused with every emotion possible. I am heartbroken for his children, who I know were everything to him, and for his family. This is such a massive loss on so many levels, words fail me.'

– Lisa Marie Presley

'I think any celebrity who met Michael Jackson was completely awed. I know I was. I kept thinking, "Oh my God, oh my God. It's him, it's him." So for me he was the celebrity of celebrities.'

— Serena Williams

'Just as there will never be another Fred Astaire or Chuck Berry or Elvis Presley, there will never be anyone comparable to Michael Jackson. His talent, his wonderment and his mystery make him legend.' — Steven Spielberg

'Michael Jackson was my musical God. He made me believe that all things are possible, and through real and positive music, he can live forever. I love Michael Jackson. God bless him.' — Wyclef Jean

'Michael was and will remain one of the greatest entertainers that ever lived. He was exceptional, artistic and original. He gave the world his heart and soul through his music.' — Berry Gordy

'With Michael's death, a legend is born that will last until the end of time.' — Shakira

BIBLIOGRAPHY

Michael Jackson: Conspiracy, Aphrodite Jones, Aphrodite Jones Books, 2007

Michael Jackson: For the Record, Chris Cadman and Craig Halstead, Authors OnLine, 2007

Michael Jackson: The Magic and the Madness, J. Randy Taraborrelli, Pan, 2004

Michael Jackson: The Visual Documentary, Adrian Grant, Omnibus Press, 2005

Moonwalk, Michael Jackson, Mandarin, 1988

Unmasked: The Final Years of Michael Jackson, Ian Halperin, Simon & Schuster, 2009

SELECT DISCOGRAPHY

Main solo albums

2008   King of Pop
2003   Number Ones
2001   Invincible
1997   Blood on the Dance Floor: HIStory in the Mix
1995   HIStory: Past, Present and Future – Book 1
1991   Dangerous
1987   Bad
1984   Farewell My Summer Love
1982   Thriller
1981   One Day in Your Life
1979   Off the Wall
1975   The Best of Michael Jackson
1975   Forever, Michael
1973   Music & Me
1972   Ben
1972   Got To Be There

Solo singles

2008   Wanna Be Startin' Somethin' 2008 (with Akon)
2008   The Girl Is Mine 2008 (with Will.I.Am)
2003   One More Chance
2002   Butterflies
2001   Cry
2001   You Rock My World
1997   HIStory/Ghosts
1997   Blood on the Dance Floor
1997   Smile
1996   Stranger in Moscow
1996   They Don't Care About Us
1996   This Time Around (with The Notorious B.I.G.)

1995	Earth Song
1995	You Are Not Alone
1995	Scream/Childhood (with Janet Jackson)
1993	Dangerous
1993	Gone Too Soon
1993	Will You Be There
1993	Give in to Me
1993	Who Is It?
1992	Heal the World
1992	Jam
1992	In the Closet
1992	Remember the Time
1991	Black or White
1989	Liberian Girl
1989	Leave Me Alone
1988	Smooth Criminal
1988	Another Part of Me
1988	Dirty Diana
1988	Man in the Mirror
1987	The Way You Make Me Feel
1987	Bad
1987	I Just Can't Stop Loving You (with Siedah Garrett)
1984	Girl You're So Together
1984	Farewell My Summer Love
1984	Thriller
1983	P.Y.T. (Pretty Young Thing)
1983	Human Nature
1983	Wanna Be Startin' Somethin'
1983	Beat It
1983	Billie Jean
1982	The Girl Is Mine (with Paul McCartney)
1981	One Day in Your Life
1980	Heartbreak Hotel
1980	Girlfriend
1980	She's Out of My Life
1980	Off the Wall
1979	Rock with You
1979	Don't Stop 'Til You Get Enough
1979	You Can't Win
1975	Just a Little Bit of You
1975	We're Almost There
1973	Happy
1973	Music and Me
1973	With a Child's Heart

1972   Ben
1972   Ain't No Sunshine
1972   I Wanna Be Where You Are
1972   Rockin' Robin
1971   Got To Be There

The Jacksons main albums

1989   2300 Jackson Street
1984   Victory
1981   The Jacksons Live!
1980   Triumph
1978   Destiny
1977   Goin' Places
1976   The Jacksons

Jackson 5 main albums

1975   Moving Violation
1974   Dancing Machine
1973   Get It Together
1973   Skywriter
1972   Lookin' Through the Windows
1971   Greatest Hits
1971   Goin' Back to Indiana
1971   Maybe Tomorrow
1970   The Jackson 5 Christmas Album
1970   Third Album
1970   ABC
1970   Diana Ross Presents The Jackson 5

The Jacksons singles

1989   Art of Madness
1989   Nothing (That Compares 2 You)
1988   2300 Jackson Street
1987   Time Out for the Burglar
1984   Wait
1984   Body
1984   Torture
1984   State of Shock
1981   Things I Do for You
1981   Time Waits for No One
1981   Walk Right Now

1981   Can You Feel It
1980   This Place Hotel
1980   Lovely One
1979   Destiny
1979   Shake Your Body (Down to the Ground)
1978   Blame It on the Boogie
1978   Find Me a Girl
1978   Music's Taking Over
1978   Different Kind of Lady
1977   Even Though You're Gone
1977   Goin' Places
1977   Dreamer
1977   Show You the Way to Go
1976   Enjoy Yourself

Jackson 5 singles

1975   All I Do Is Think of You
1975   Forever Came Today
1974   I Am Love
1974   Life of the Party
1974   Whatever You've Got I Want
1974   Dancing machine
1974   The Boogie Man
1973   Get It Together
1973   Skywriter
1973   Hallelujah Day
1972   Corner of the Sky
1972   Doctor My Eyes
1972   Lookin' Through the Windows
1972   Little Bitty Pretty One
1971   Sugar Daddy
1971   Maybe Tomorrow
1971   Never Can Say Goodbye
1971   Mama's Pearl
1970   I Saw Mommy Kissing Santa Claus
1970   Santa Claus Is Coming to Town
1970   I'll Be There
1970   The Love You Save
1970   ABC
1969   I Want You Back
1968   Big Boy/You've Changed

(The initials JJ, KJ and MJ in subentries denote Joseph, Katherine and Michael Jackson.)